Milton Whitney, Amory Austin

Rice:

Its cultivation, production, and distribution in the United States and

foreign countries - Vol. 6

Milton Whitney, Amory Austin

Rice:
Its cultivation, production, and distribution in the United States and foreign countries - Vol. 6

ISBN/EAN: 9783337775322

Printed in Europe, USA, Canada, Australia, Japan

Cover: Foto ©ninafisch / pixelio.de

More available books at **www.hansebooks.com**

U. S. DEPARTMENT OF AGRICULTURE.

DIVISION OF STATISTICS.

MISCELLANEOUS SERIES. REPORT No. 6.

RICE:

ITS CULTIVATION, PRODUCTION, AND DISTRIBUTION

IN THE

UNITED STATES AND FOREIGN COUNTRIES.

PREPARED UNDER THE DIRECTION OF THE STATISTICIAN

BY

AMORY AUSTIN, B. S.

WITH A CHAPTER ON THE RICE SOILS OF SOUTH CAROLINA
BY MILTON WHITNEY, M. S.

PUBLISHED BY AUTHORITY OF THE SECRETARY OF AGRICULTURE.

WASHINGTON:
GOVERNMENT PRINTING OFFICE.
1893.

LETTER OF TRANSMITTAL.

U. S. DEPARTMENT OF AGRICULTURE,
DIVISION OF STATISTICS,
Washington, D. C., January 23, 1893.

SIR: I respectfully submit for publication, as Report No. 6 of our miscellaneous statistical series, a report upon the cultivation, production, and distribution of rice in the United States and foreign countries, which has been prepared in this office, under my direction, by Mr. Amory Austin. A chapter is added relative to the characteristics of the rice soils of South Carolina, by Prof. Milton Whitney, of Johns Hopkins University.

Respectfully,

J. R. DODGE,
Statistician.

Hon. J. M. RUSK,
Secretary.

3

CONTENTS.

RICE: ITS CULTIVATION, PRODUCTION, AND DIS-TRIBUTION IN THE UNITED STATES AND FOR-EIGN COUNTRIES.

INTRODUCTORY.

Among cereals and grains rice unquestionably stands first in importance in regard to the number of persons who consume it, the area devoted to its cultivation, and the amount annually produced thereon in the whole world. It has been stated that rice forms the principal, and in some cases almost the only, food of from one-third to one-half the whole human race, a statement which can not be made of any other edible product, except perhaps of meat. China and its dependencies have a population of about 404,000,000, or 27.5 per cent of the total population of the globe, and rice certainly forms the principal food supply of its people. The same may be said of India, with its population of 273,000,000, or 18.6 per cent of the total population. Statistics have shown that in Japan, which has a population of 39,000,000, rice forms 51 per cent of the total sustenance. The population of the principal remaining rice-consuming countries of Asia and Africa may be roughly estimated at about 80,000,000, and the total of the above figures reaches the sum of 796,000,000 people, or 54.2 per cent of the total population of the earth, which in 1890 * was estimated at 1,468,000,000.

The Americas, Europe, and Australia do not enter into the above enumeration, since, although the cultivation of rice receives great attention and the rice itself is extensively consumed in all of these divisions, it can not be said to be one of the principal sources of food supply, its place being rather taken by wheat, rye, maize, and other cereals.

Rice has been known from the earliest historical times. It is mentioned in the Talmud, though neither in the Old nor in the New Testament; it was certainly known to the Romans, was mentioned in the Tragedies of Sophocles, the Greek poet, B. C. 495, and was described and named by the Greek philosopher Theophrastus, about B. C. 300. Legend places its introduction into China in the year B. C. 2822, and it is known to have been cultivated in Java as early as A. D. 1084.

The native country of rice is not known with certainty. Linnæus places it in Ethiopia; the traveler Barth saw rice growing wild in

---

* Statesman's Year Book for 1891.

7

Central Africa in 1857; others regard it as having been native in Asia. The Danish traveler Klein mentions having found rice growing wild in India, but it has never been proved that what he saw had not been brought there by man. According to some authorities rice is indigenous to eastern South America and is found in a native state upon the Amazon, though this statement has not been confirmed. It does not seem to be native in North America, even in the more tropical regions. It seems highly probable that rice is native to eastern India and the islands of the Malay Archipelago. From these localities it seems to have spread over eastern and southern Asia, and westwardly to Persia and Arabia. From Arabia it spread over Egypt and northern Africa, and was carried by the Arabs to Sicily, and by the Moors to Spain. It is said to have been introduced into northern Italy by the armies of Charles V. in 1521, and thence into southern France.

Its earliest introduction into our own country is said to have been in 1647, when Sir William Berkeley, governor of Virginia, caused a half bushel of seed (in all likelihood brought from England, whither it had been carried from India) to be planted in that colony, which is recorded as having yielded a crop of 16 bushels of good rice.

The important introduction of rice into this country, however, was at Charleston, S. C., in the year 1694. An English or Dutch ship, homeward bound from Madagascar, was driven by stress of weather to seek shelter in the harbor of Charleston, and the captain seized the opportunity to visit an old acquaintance, the landgrave and governor of the province, Thomas Smith, whom he had already met in Madagascar. Smith expressed the desire to experiment with the growing of rice upon a low, moist patch of ground in his garden, similar to ground upon which he had seen rice growing in Madagascar, whereupon the captain presented him with a small bag of rice seed which happened to be among the ship's stores. The seed was planted in the garden in Longitude Lane, Charleston, the spot being still pointed out, and thus was originated the important industry of rice cultivation, still flourishing in South Carolina.* There is a story also that the Earl of Shaftsbury sent 100 pounds of the seed to Charleston about the same time, from the produce of which a cargo of 60 tons of paddy was shipped to England in 1698. Lowland rice was introduced into Louisiana in 1718, and upland rice into South Carolina in 1772, coming, it is said, from Cochin China. The rice which came from Madagascar in 1694 had in all probability been carried to that island from Egypt or from India.

Thus this plant from its Asiatic birthplace has made the circuit of the earth and is now cultivated throughout the torrid zone and in the warmer parts of both temperate zones wherever there is an abundant supply of water. Its geographical limits are given from 45° N. to 38° S. latitude in the Eastern and from 36° N. to 38° S. latitude in the Western Hemisphere.

---

* Ramsay's " History of South Carolina."

Rice is an annual plant belonging to the natural order of the grasses, genus *Oryza* (Linnæus). Many varieties and subvarieties of it are known, the chief difference appearing to be in the size, shape, and color of the grain, due to variations in soil, climate, and method of cultivation. Thus, a botanical catalogue enumerates 161 varieties found in Ceylon alone, while in Japan, China, and India, where its cultivation has gone on for centuries, and where great care is usually taken in the improvement of the crop by selection of seed, no less than 1,400 varieties are said to exist. Practically, however, these may be classed under two principal species, as follows: (1) The common lowland rice (*Oryza sativa*), which is essentially a marsh plant and requires an abundant supply of water for successful growth and a temperature of from 60° to 80° F. for ripening. It flourishes best near the level of the sea, but it will, under favorable circumstances, do well at higher altitudes. It resembles oats in some of its characteristics, and has both beardless and barbed varieties. *O. præcox* is an early variety of the *sativa*, which it otherwise closely resembles, being a semiaquatic or marsh-loving plant. (2) The upland or mountain rice (*O. mutica*) is generally less productive than the preceding, and grows in comparatively dry soils, often at considerable altitudes. This variety is now cultivated in many places in the interior of Europe, and there is reason to believe that it will thrive wherever maize will ripen. A hardy variety (*O. nepalensis*) is said to be found in a wild state near the snow line of the Himalayas. It is also said that although lowland rice may be successfully raised upon uplands, mountain rice will not grow well upon lowlands or marshes, and that an amount of irrigation sufficient for lowland rice will prove injurious or even fatal to the upland variety. Upland rice is supposed to have originally been a native of Java or Ceylon.

Intermediate between lowland and upland rice is a peculiar variety (*Oryza glutinosa*, or clammy rice), principally found in Japan and India, which has the property of yielding a viscous mass when boiled with water. This is due to the more or less complete replacement of the natural starch of the grain by dextrine, which is soluble in water. The grain of this rice, when treated with a solution of iodine, gives a reddish-brown color, characteristic of dextrine, instead of the dark blue color afforded by ordinary rice-starch. The Japanese cultivate this variety under the name of *Motsi*. *O. latifolia* is a broad leaved variety of lowland rice indigenous to Brazil.

"Wild-rice," also known as "Indian rice," "Canada rice," or "Water oats" (*Zizani aquatica*), is not a rice at all, though it bears some resemblance to the *Oryza*, and is botanically related to it. It is widely diffused over North America, both in inland districts and near the sea, and is also found in eastern Siberia and Japan. It is especially abundant in the Upper Lake Region of the United States and Canada, where it covers areas often miles in extent, growing in the rich black mud of the river banks or along the margins and outlets of the lakes, in from 4 to 12 feet of water, rising above the surface of the water to a height of from 4 to 6 feet, with its roots but slightly attached to the mud beneath. The banks of the St. Croix River and the small lakes of Minnesota are particularly favorable to its growth.

The Zizania is an annual, though often erroneously called a perennial. The ripe seed is shaken off from the panicle with the slightest agitation caused by wind or wave and sinks to the muddy bed below, where it remains during the winter, germinating and growing in the spring, while the old plant dies and disappears. The wild rice thus appears as a perennial and as if growing year by year from the same root, while in reality it is a self-sowing annual.

The plant has a thick, spongy stem, with long, broad leaves. The grain is larger than that of ordinary rice, is dark in color, and has a closely adhering husk; it is palatable and nutritious, and when it ripens, in September or October, immense flocks of wild ducks and ricebirds are attracted to the regions where it grows. It has been estimated that an acre of wild rice is equivalent in nutriment to an acre of wheat.

This plant would be of great economic value could it be domesticated; not only might it furnish food for man, but the grain would be exceedingly valuable for feeding poultry, while the leaves would afford a nutritious forage for cattle. Unfortunately, however, all attempts at cultivation have hitherto failed, principally on account of the tendency of the plant to drop its seed at the moment of ripening.

The Sioux, Chippewas, and other Indian tribes formerly made extensive use of this grain as a food supply, gathering it by the aid of canoes and husking it, after parching over a slow fire, by simple treading with the bare feet. In England attempts have been made to utilize its straw as a paper stock, though without any very notable results.

A variety of wild rice (Z. miliacea or "folle avoine"), doubtfully said to be a true perennial, is found all over the Southern States, but principally in the bayous of Louisiana. Two crops of good hay may be cut from it yearly, but its grain does not seem to have been utilized.

As a food material rice is nutritious and easily digestible. In comparison with other grains it is poor in nitrogenous substances (albuminoids) and in fatty matters, and correspondingly rich in nonnitrogenous substances (carbohydrates). The following analyses of various kinds of rice, and of certain other cereals and food materials, are taken from Köenig's Nahrungs- und Genuss-mittel, 1889, and from the Fourth Annual Report of the Storrs Experiment Station, 1891, and will serve to illustrate the value of rice as a food material:

TABLE I.—*Analyses of rice and certain other cereals and food materials.*

[Taken from Köenig's Nahrungs- und Genuss-mittel, 1889.]

Substance examined.	In the original substance.						In the dried substance.			
	Water.	Albuminoids.	Fats.	Carbohydrates.	Fiber.	Ash.	Albuminoids.	Carbohydrates.	Nitrogen.	
	P. ct.	P. ct.	P. ct.	P. ct.	P. ct.	P. ct.	P. ct.	P. ct.	P. ct.	
Paddy	14.42	6.93	2.41	61.18	9.73	5.33	8.09	71.52	1.29	Grandeau; 1876; variety not stated.
Do	9.55	5.87	1.84	72.75	5.80	4.19	6.49	80.04	1.04	De Leeuw; 1881; variety not stated.
Carolina rice, cleaned.	11.15	7.70	0.86	78.50	0.80	0.90	8.66	88.45	0.39	Richardson; U. S. Dept. Agriculture; 1886.
Piedmont rice, cleaned.	14.60	7.50	0.50	76.00	0.90	0.50	8.69	89.08	1.39	Boussignault; 1837.
Patua rice, cleaned.	9.80	7.22	0.09	81.81	0.18	0.90	8.00	90.70	1.28	Polson; 1855.
Japan upland rice, cleaned.	12.58	7.65	2.25	74.77	1.72	1.03	8.75	85.53	1.40	Kellner; mean of 2 analyses; 1884.
American rice, cleaned.	12.40	7.40	0.40	79.20	0.20	0.40	8.44	90.41	1.35	Jenkins; mean of 10 analyses; 1884.
O. glutinosa	13.88	6.67	2.35	72.97	2.99	1.14	7.75	84.73	1.24	Kellner and Kreusler; 5 analyses; 1884.
Z. aquatica	12.00	6.74	0.70	79.63	1.93	1.70	7.74	87.29	1.24	E. Peters; 1862.
Rice cleaned	12.58	6.73	0.88	78.48	0.51	0.82	7.70	89.78	1.23	Mean of 41 analyses of all varieties.
Wheat	13.37	12.04	1.85	63.65	2.31	1.78	13.90	79.24	2.22	Mean of 948 analyses of winter and summer wheat.
Rye	13.37	10.81	1.77	70.21	1.78	2.06	12.48	81.04	2.00	Mean of 173 analyses.
Oats	12.11	10.66	4.99	58.37	10.58	3.29	12.13	66.41	1.94	Mean of 377 analyses.
Maize	13.35	9.36	4.96	68.05	2.21	1.47	11.50	78.53	1.84	Mean of 76 analyses.
Potatoes	74.98	2.08	0.15	21.07	0.69	1.09	8.33	83.92	1.33	Mean of 204 analyses.
Beef, moderately fat.	53.05	16.75	29.28	0.00	0.00	0.92	35.68	0.00	5.67	7 analyses; 62.36 per cent fat in dried substance.
Beef, lean	72.03	20.96	5.41	0.46	0.00	1.14	74.95	1.64	12.00	42 analyses; 19.33 per cent fat in dried substance.
Peas	13.92	23.15	1.89	52.63	5.68	2.68	26.89	61.21	4.30	Mean of 72 analyses of all varieties.
Beans	13.49	25.31	1.68	48.33	8.06	3.13	29.26	55.86	4.08	Mean of 63 analyses of all varieties.
Soja hispida	9.89	33.41	17.68	29.31	4.67	5.10	37.08	19.57	5.93	Mean of 25 analyses of yellow variety.

TABLE II.—*Analyses of rice and certain other cereals and food materials.*

[Taken from the Fourth Annual Report of the Storrs School Agricultural Experiment Station, Storrs, Conn., 1891.]

Substance.	Water.	Total nutriment.	Protein.	Fats.	Carbohydrates.	Mineral matter.	Fuel value.	
	Per ct.	Per ct.	Per ct.	Per ct.	Per ct.	Per ct.		
Rice, cleaned	12.40	87.60	7.40	0.40	79.40	0.40	1630	Mean of 10 analyses.*
Wheat flour	12.50	87.50	11.00	1.10	74.90	0.50	1645	Mean of 22 analyses.*
Rye flour	13.10	86.90	6.70	0.80	78.70	0.70	1625	Mean of 4 analyses.*
Oat meal	7.80	92.20	14.70	7.10	68.40	2.00	1845	Mean of 6 analyses.*
Maize meal	15.00	85.00	9.20	3.80	70.60	1.40	1645	Mean of 77 analyses.*
Potatoes	78.90	21.10	2.10	0.10	17.90	1.60	375	Mean of 12 analyses.*
Beef side, without kidney fat.	54.80	45.20	17.20	27.10	0.00	0.90	1965	Single analyses, test showing normal composition of beef.
Beef, rib	48.10	51.90	15.40	35.60	0.00	0.90	1790	Single of 5.

* The fuel value represents the number of calories of potential energy in 1 pound of the substance.

In Table I the first nine analyses show the composition of various kinds of rice, while the latter part of the table contains the means of many analyses of rice, wheat, and other important grains, together with those of potatoes, beef, and some leguminous plants for comparison. We have from these means the following figures:

	Rice	Wheat.	Rye.	Oats.	Maize.	Potatoes.	Fat beef.	Lean beef.	Soja.
	Per ct.	Per ct.	Per ct.	Per ct.	Per ct.	Per ct.	Per ct.	Per ct.	Per ct.
Albuminoids	6.73	12.04	10.81	10.66	9.36	2.08	16.75	20.96	33.41
Fatty matters	0.88	1.85	1.77	4.99	4.96	0.15	29.28	5.41	17.68
Carbohydrates	78.48	68.65	70.21	58.37	68.65	21.01	None.	0.46	29.31
Total nutritive matter.	86.09	82.54	82.79	74.02	82.97	23.24	46.03	26.83	80.40

These figures show that rice contains a slightly larger amount of total nutritive matter than wheat or rye, the exact proportion being 1 pound of rice equivalent to 1.043 pounds of wheat or to 1.040 pounds of rye. Maize approaches rice somewhat more nearly, the proportion of rice to maize being as 1 to 1.038. Rice is more nutritious than whole oats, 1 pound of the former being equivalent to 1.163 pounds of the latter, while it contains 3.70 times as much nutritive matter as potatoes, 1.87 times as much as fat beef, and 3.21 times as much as lean or good ordinary beef.

In Table II the relative proportions are much the same, 1 pound of ice being equivalent in total nutriment to almost exactly 1 pound of wheat flour, or to very little more than a pound of rye flour, while the proportion of rice to maize meal is as 1 to 1.036; to potatoes as 1 to 4.171; to the normal composition of beef (as expressed in the analysis of meat from a whole side, the kidney fat being excluded) as 1 to 1.938; and to the meat of rib beef as 1 to 1.688. In this table rice is shown to be less nutritious than oatmeal in the proportion of 1 part of the former to 0.95 part of the latter. The meal is more nutritious than whole oats, owing to the removal of most of the 10 per cent of fiber or husk which the rice grain is shown to contain in Table I.

Table II also shows the fuel value of these food materials. This value is an expression of the capacity of a food to furnish heat and muscular energy to the body, and is calculated from the chemical composition of the food, the specific energy of albuminoids, fatty matters, and carbohydrates being known. The unit of measurement is the calorie, or amount of heat which will raise the temperature of a kilogramme of water through 1 degree of the Centigrade thermometer, or, in more familiar terms, which will make a pound of water 4 Fahrenheit degrees warmer. One calorie corresponds to 1.53 foot tons, i. e., to 1.53 times the amount of labor or muscular force which will raise the weight of a ton of 2,240 pounds to the height of 1 foot. Knowing, then, the specific energy of 1 gram of the albuminoids or carbohydrates to be equivalent to 4.1 calories, and of 1 gram of fatty food to be equivalent to 9.3 calories, as has been established by experiment, we have all the data necessary for calculating the fuel value or potential energy of each variety of food and for comparing the results. Thus, in the above table, it is shown that a pound of rice is slightly less energetic than a pound of wheat, or slightly more so than a pound of rye flour or of maize meal; also, that a pound of rice is less energetic than a pound of rib beef, which is fat, but more so than a pound of lean side beef; it is considerably less energetic than a pound of oatmeal, but has more than four times the energy of a pound of potatoes. This subject has been fully discussed in a paper by Prof. W. O. Atwater, in the Third Annual Report of the Storrs Station, 1890.

The actual value of rice or of any other substance as a food depends not only upon the relative amount of nutriment which it contains, but also upon the kind of nutriment. An examination of the above tables will show that rice is essentially a nonnitrogenous food. It contains on an average from 6.50 to 7.75 per cent of nitrogenous or albuminoid (protein) substances, such as gluten, which forms muscle, blood, and bone in the body, whereas other grains, such as wheat, oats, or maize, contain from 9 to 15 per cent of such substances. On the other hand, it contains a larger proportion of nonnitrogenous substances or carbohydrates, such as starch, which are heat producing and which are transformed in the animal economy into fats; of these it contains, on the average, from 70 to 80 per cent, while other cereals contain from 60 to 70 per cent only. Rice is thus a nonnitrogenous, heat-producing, and fattening food, and must be supplemented by a more nitrogenous and muscle-building food in order that those persons who habitually consume it shall receive a fair proportion of nutriment of both kinds, such as is essential to their general health and well being. This is provided for as follows: In Asiatic countries, where rice forms the main article of food, many leguminous vegetables, principally peas and beans (pulse), are also eaten in large quantities. In Table I it will be seen that both of these vegetables are rich in nitrogenous matters, the former containing an average of 23.15 per cent, and the latter of 25.31 per cent. In southern India similar use is made of the natchnee or ragi (*Eleusine indica*, or *E. coracana*), the grain of which is highly nitrogenous. In Japan, in addition to fish, which is a favorite food among all classes, great use is made of the *Soja hispida*, a leguminous plant closely resembling the pea or bean, and found native in the country in several varieties. This vegetable is extremely nitrogenous, containing from 32 to 40 per cent of albuminoids, and being, according to the above analysis, nearly equal to wheat in nutritive value, 1 pound of rice being equivalent to 1.043 pounds of wheat, or to 1.070 pounds of *soja;* 1 pound of soja is equivalent to 1.75 pounds of fat, or to 3 pounds of lean beef. Thus, in these countries, leguminous plants well supplement a rice diet, and take the place occupied by meat, fish, milk, cheese, etc., in European countries and in America.

Rice is easily digestible. The following table of digestibility is abridged from one compiled by Profs. Atwater and Woods in Bulletin No. 7 of the Storrs Experiment Station, September, 1891. The totals for the first four materials are the same as those given in Table II, and the author's remark that the digestion coefficients used are reasonably accurate (considering the difficulty of exact determinations), except in the case of the fats. The table shows rice to be fully as digestible as

TABLE III.—*Proportions of nutrients digested and not digested from food materials by healthy men.*

Materials.	Protein, or albuminoids.			Fats.			Carbohydrates.		
	Digested.	Undigested.	Total.	Digested.	Undigested.	Total.	Digested.	Undigested.	Total.
	Per ct.	Per ct.	Per ct.	Per ct.	Per ct.	Per ct.	Per ct.	Per ct.	Per ct.
Rice, cleaned	6.30	1.10	7.40	0.30	0.10	0.40	75.40	4.00	79.40
Wheat flour, fine	9.40	1.60	11.00	0.90	0.20	1.10	71.10	3.80	74.90
Maize meal	7.80	1.40	9.20	3.00	0.80	3.80	67.10	3.50	70.60
Potatoes	1.60	0.50	2.10	(?)	(?)	0.10	17.00	0.90	17.90
Wheat bread	7.10	1.70	8.80	1.40	0.30	1.70	53.40	2.80	56.20
Beef, sirloin	18.50	....	18.50	14.80	0.80	15.60	....	....	....
Mutton, shoulder	18.10	....	18.10	21.30	1.10	22.40	....	....	....
Pork, very fat	0.90	....	0.90	78.70	4.10	82.80	....	....	....
Codfish, fresh	15.80	....	15.80	0.40	....	0.40	....	....	....
Eggs	14.90	....	14.90	10.30	0.20	10.50	....	....	....
Milk	3.60	....	3.60	3.80	0.20	4.00	4.70	....	4.70

wheat flour or Indian meal and more so than bread or potatoes, while in common with all cereal or vegetable foods it is less digestible than meat or other animal foods.

Digestion coefficients.—Eighty-five per cent of the protein or albuminoids is digested in rice, fine wheat flour, and maize meal; 80 per cent in wheat bread, and 75 per cent in potatoes; in all these substances the coefficients of 80 per cent for fats and 95 per cent for carbohydrates is assumed. Of beef, mutton, pork, and fish 100 per cent, or the total protein, is digested, as well as 95 per cent of the fats. In the case of eggs, 100 per cent of the protein and 98 per cent of the fats are digested, and in milk the total protein and carbohydrates (milk sugar), with 96 per cent of the fats.

An experiment made at the Agricultural Experiment Station of the University of Louisiana with artificial gastric juice (an acidulated aqueous solution of pepsin) showed 83.11 per cent of the albuminoids of cleaned rice to be digestible.[*] It is said that boiled rice is digestible in one hour, while the same amount of roast beef requires three hours for digestion. New rice, it is said, produces indigestion, and it should not be used until at least six months old. In India rice is sometimes kept for three years before using.

Rice is used for food in all forms, the grains being whole, broken, or ground. The usual method of cooking it is by boiling in water, though in some Asiatic countries it is simply parched or roasted, whereby part of its starch is converted into dextrine. Strange to say, except in the Southern States, the proper method of cooking rice does not seem to be understood in this country. It comes to the table as an uninviting, glutinous mass, instead of being, as it should be, one of the most appetizing dishes in appearance, with each snow-white grain dis-

[*] Bulletin No. 24, Rice and its By-Products, Baton Rouge, 1889.

tinct and separate from the rest. The great secret of the proper cooking of rice lies in allowing plenty of water, yet not too much; in not boiling for too long a time, and in not breaking the grains by stirring during the time of boiling. The rice should be washed in three or four changes of water to remove adhering rice flour, dust, etc., and should be boiled only until the grain is well softened; after this the water should be poured off, the vessel tightly closed, and the rice allowed to steam. A Japanese authority gives the amount of water to be used as from 2 to 2.12 liters for 1.80 liters of rice, and says that the rice should be put into water which has been previously boiled and is still hot; cooking, he says, occupies from fifteen to twenty-five minutes. An Australian writer states that the rice in boiling absorbs three times its weight of water, so that plenty of water should be used, while other experts say that too much water is apt to make the rice pasty.

Since rice contains almost 80 per cent of starch and but little gluten, its flour is not readily panificable, and does not undergo fermentation with yeast; hence, rice flour can not be used alone for making bread, though it may be so used when mixed with wheat flour. Its starch may, however, be readily converted into glucose, and hence rice is much used for distillation. In the United Kingdom 2,886 tons of rice were used for this purpose in 1889. The natives of India make a strong spirituous liquor from rice, "arrack," containing about 50 per cent, by weight, of alcohol. The Japanese "saki," a sort of beer made from rice, contains about 12.50 per cent of alcohol.

One of the principal uses of rice is for the extraction of its starch, which is of extreme fineness and much in demand for certain purposes to which ordinary wheat starch or potato starch is not so well adapted. Rice meal is found to be highly nutritious for live stock, especially for swine, and paddy or unhusked rice is especially good for poultry. Not much use can be made of rice straw, except as a fertilizer, since it is large and soft and is ill adapted to the uses generally made of ordinary straw. It is said that it does not even make a good litter for cattle, although when well rotted it makes an excellent manure for maize and potatoes. The chaff or husk of rice is also valuable as a fertilizer, especially as it aids in keeping the soil open and porous. The so-called "rice straw," used for hat-making, etc., is, in reality, a very fine rye or wheat straw expressly grown for the purpose and obtained by sowing these cereals very thickly upon light alluvial soil, the grain produced being, in this case, of secondary moment. Finally, the so-called "rice paper" of the Chinese is not made from rice, but is manufactured from the pith of *Aralia* (*Fatsia*) papyrifera, a tree native to the island of Formosa.

RICE IN THE UNITED STATES.

Rice is grown within a very limited area in the United States, comprising certain lands along the Atlantic coast south of the parallel of 36° north latitude, and other tracts bordering upon the Gulf of Mexico, in the States of North Carolina, South Carolina, Georgia, Florida, Alabama, Mississippi, Louisiana, and Texas. The amount of rice produced in this country suffices for little more than half the amount annually consumed, and could the production be increased, as has been suggested, by substituting the cultivation of rice for that of cotton, now overproduced, great benefit would result therefrom. There is no reason why the United States should not produce the largest rice crop in the world. Both lowland and upland rice are grown in this area, the former mostly along the coasts and the latter in the inland districts.

There are several varieties of lowland rice, the most appreciated being the gold seed, so called from the golden yellow color of its husk when ripe. Of this, again, there are two subvarieties, or more properly two sizes, the smaller of which was introduced into the country a few years before the Revolutionary war, and the larger about the year 1840. The principal difference between the two is but a slight one in the length of the grain, and they are otherwise hardly distinguishable in size, and differ but little as to yield or quality. The gold seed rice has almost entirely superseded the white rice, which was formerly used, and it has of late years undergone such improvements, through careful selection of seed and very attentive cultivation, that it is now the most important rice of American commerce. The famous Carolina rice is esteemed, especially among foreign consumers, as the best rice in the world. White rice, a lowland variety, was the original rice introduced in 1694. It has a cream-colored husk, and resembles that commonly grown in China. It is valued on account of its precocity, and, like the gold seed, succeeds almost as well upon the uplands as upon the coast.

Measurements of grains of gold seed and white rice, made in 1854, gave the following figures:

	Length of the grain.	Circumference around shorter axis.	Number of grains in one Troy ounce.
	Inches.	*Inches.*	
Gold seed, long grain	0.417	0.375	841
Gold seed, short grain	0.375	0.375	896
White rice	0.375	0.375	960

Experimental planting also shows the long-grained to be but slightly more prolific than the short-grained variety. A bearded variety, the awn of which was very long, was at one time experimented with upon the uplands, but did not prove satisfactory and was abandoned.

SOUTH CAROLINA.

For two centuries this State has remained preëminent in rice cultivation in America. The rice which came from Madagascar two hundred years ago found a congenial soil and climate at Charleston, and so thrived that its cultivation extended to the adjoining colonies and became a lucrative branch of agriculture. It is recorded that in 1754 the colony exported to England over 100,000 barrels of unhusked rice, and had an ample supply left for home consumption. This yield might have been much greater had the system of water culture, now in use, been practiced at that time, but this was not introduced until thirty years later, in 1784.

Although rice is cultivated for local consumption in almost every part of South Carolina and Georgia below actual mountain altitudes, the more important rice fields, where the commercial crop is grown, are mainly confined to the swamps and tide-water lands along the coast. There are also many of the best rice plantations among the swamp lands higher up the rivers, and upon level lands in the interior so situated as to be readily irrigated. Upon all these lands the system of water cultivation is the one generally followed. The tide-water lands lie along the rivers in such position above the meeting of fresh and salt water that they may be flooded by fresh water at high tide, and drained when the tide is low, yet may be protected by means of dikes from salt water (always fatal to rice) coming from below, or from freshets coming from above. In certain localities lands have even been reclaimed from the salt marshes, and these are said to be among the very best of all rice fields.

Some of these tide-water lands are said to have been valued at from $200 to $300 per acre before the late war, but in addition to the almost total destruction of rice cultivation caused by the war, recovery from which is not even yet complete, the present difficulty of obtaining labor has reduced the price of these lands to not more than $20 to $30 per acre. The soil is alluvial and generally consists of a blue or yellow clay, containing much mica.

Among the river swamps lands are chosen for rice fields which are so situated that they may be readily flooded with water from the river above, and drained into the river again at a lower level. It is said that many such situations are to be found in almost every part of the State, and that there are some 2,000,000 acres of such lands, or good tidal lands, lying idle which are eminently adapted for rice cultivation. Much good rice land may also be found among the inland swamps. These swamps are large shallow basins, and have streams or "water leads" running into them. They may easily be reclaimed by drainage and may be so arranged as to be readily irrigated, reservoirs to hold a supply of water from the streams being generally easy of construction in these localities. Such lands, however, have a heavier soil than the tidal lands, and are in consequence more difficult to cultivate, and they are neither so prolific nor so remunerative. The grain grown upon them is heavy and gives less return per acre than that grown along the river, and yet with care and proper management a profit may be made.

The rice fields are surrounded by embankments both along the river front and upon their inland boundaries. These embankments are made

14257—No. 6——2

of sufficient height and strength to exclude the salt-water tides and the water from the river, but are provided with flood gates at proper intervals, so arranged as to be under complete control. The whole area of the fields is subdivided by smaller embankments or dikes into sections containing from 15 to 20 acres each, and these sections are again subdivided, by means of canals and ditches, into beds of from 20 to 30 feet in width. The whole area is generally traversed by a large main canal, from 12 to 30 feet wide and from 4 to 5 feet deep, which answers the double purpose of conducting the water to the fields or of draining them, as may be necessary, and of affording a means of communication by boats in harvest time. This canal communicates directly, through flood gates, with the river or main source of water supply.

It is of extreme importance that rice lands should be perfectly level, in order that during cultivation the depth of water upon the fields may be the same throughout, so that one part of the crop may receive the same treatment as another. The tidal lands and swamp areas are already level by nature, and in other places inequalities must be reduced and the surface made uniform. In some countries terracing is resorted to when practicable. All bowlders, stones, stumps, etc., must be removed from the fields, especially among the inland swamps, and all irregularities of surface must be reduced and the whole fashioned into a perfectly level plain.

SYSTEM OF CULTIVATION.

The system of water cultivation for lowland rice as practiced in South Carolina, and as generally adopted in all the rice-growing States, is as follows:

Operations are commenced as soon as the previous harvest has been gathered and removed, which is in September or early in October. The first thing done is to thoroughly clear out the ditches and drains, removing the mud and refuse down to hard soil below. In some localities, however, the drains alone are cleared every year, while it is considered necessary to clear the ditches once in three or four years. The embankments and dikes are next inspected and put in thorough order for the coming season. Plowing is the next operation, and in order that the clods shall have the full benefit of the frost, this is done as early in the winter as possible; only a slight plowing of 4 or 5 inches, or just enough to turn the stubble under, is necessary, as these soils are constantly being enriched by alluvial deposits from the water used in their cultivation. It is found advantageous to flood the fields in cold weather with a shallow layer of water, which is then suddenly drawn off, so that the ground may freeze and the furrow-slices be broken up. The floods should not be too deep, since the weight of the water would pack the soil together and thus the effect of plowing would be counteracted, while subsequent harrowing would be rendered more difficult. Harrowing is not commenced until just before the time of planting, in order that the seed bed may be freshly prepared, and thus encourage germination and permit the young roots to expand rapidly in the loose soil and become firmly fixed. Harrowing also affords the best opportunity for killing weeds and grasses. Every clod should be broken up, the hoe being used if necessary, and the weeds and grasses allowed to wither. A crusher is then used to bring the soil to as perfect a state of tilth as possible, after which it is ready to receive the seed.

Planting occurs from the middle of March to the middle of May, according to the state of the season. The amount of seed, which should be carefully selected and free from all impurities, is from $2\frac{1}{2}$ to 3 bushels (about 45 pounds to the bushel) per acre, the greater quantity being used when the field is not at its best state of preparation. Broadcast sowing is never practiced upon these fields, but the seed is sown in drills or small furrows 2 or 3 inches deep, from 3 to 5 inches wide, and placed from 12 to 15 inches apart.

There are two systems of planting, each of which has its advocates. The first of these is known as the "covered rice" system, where the seed is sown in the drills and immediately covered with the soil to a depth of 2 or 3 inches, whereby it is protected from the attacks of birds and from floating away when the water is let on. The second system is known as that of the "open trench," in which the same drills are used and the seed is planted in the same way and in the same proportions per acre, but is not covered with soil, the drills being left open. In order to prevent the seed from floating away it is weighted by being soaked in thick clay-water before planting. This system is not a favorite one in South Carolina and is rarely practiced by the best planters, and seems to have as its only advantages the saving of a little time and labor and the hastening of germination. It is open to many objections, not the least of which is the liability to depredation by birds. In very clayey lands, however, it is sometimes advantageous.

The sowing of the entire field having been completed, irrigation is commenced and the first flooding or "sprout water" is allowed to enter. If the "covered rice" system has been followed and the soil is already moist, the water may be let in rapidly until it has attained a depth of from 12 to 18 inches, when all the flood gates are closed and the water allowed to remain stationary at this depth. Much light refuse or trash will now float and should be immediately raked out of the water before it becomes soaked and settles upon the seed. In from three to six days, according to the weather, the grain will germinate, when the water must be drawn off and the field kept as dry as possible until the young plants have grown strong enough to be independent of the support of the mother seed, that is, until they have put out two green leaves, and may be seen in this condition over the entire bed. Until this occurs the roots of the plant are not yet strong enough to fix it firmly to the soil, and were the beds covered with water the slightest agitation from the wind or other causes would uproot it.

If the "open trench" system has been followed the "sprout flow" should not be admitted rapidly into the field at first, as the force of the water would dislodge the seed, but the water should be allowed to trickle slowly in until the soil is thoroughly saturated, and the seed adheres to the ground, when the gates may be opened wider and the water let in more rapidly until the above depth of 12 to 18 inches is attained. The water is then held stationary until the rice plants are well sprouted or until signs of floating are perceptible, when it must be very carefully drawn off. Here all difference between the two systems of planting comes to an end, and the cultivation is continued as follows:

As soon as the rice plants have two leaves the second flooding or "long point flow" takes place. This is counted as one continuous flow, lasting from the rooting of the young plants until the period of dry growth, though the level of the water is once or twice changed, and the water, should occasion require it, is completely drawn off, though never for more than a day at a time.

At first the water is allowed to flow in to the same depth as before— 12 or 18 inches, and completely submerges the plants. Should there be very much grass upon the beds this flow may be advanced a day or two, though it is better to have removed as much of the grass as possible while the field is still dry. The water is kept at the above depth for about seven days in warm, or ten days in cooler weather, but not so long as to weaken the plant and cause it to fall when unsupported by water. Any trash which rises to the surface must be removed. The level of the water is then very gradually reduced until the tops of the plants appear above the surface, which will be at a depth of about 6 inches. If the fields are level and have been well prepared, and the previous cultivation has been well conducted, the plants should now be of about uniform height all over the field, and here the importance of having the field perfectly level is seen, since, if it is too low in one part the rice will suffer from too great a weight of water, and if too high in another the grass will not be so thoroughly killed.

The water is then kept at this reduced level for from sixty to sixty-five days, the level being rigorously maintained, and this time being reckoned from the commencement of the "long point flow." During this time the rice grows vigorously, and the last of the grass dies. On or about the fifteenth day of this growth a critical period occurs when the rice is apt to suddenly stop growing. If left to itself it will put forth new roots and soon resume its growth, whereas if any attempt be made to better it by drawing off the water, it may result in serious injury, the rice becoming "foxed."

At this time the rice is liable to the attack of the water weevil, which thrives if the water be stale. The remedy is, therefore, to drain off the field, letting it remain dry for a day or two, and replacing the water to the same level as before, carefully avoiding, of course, the critical period of the plant's growth, above mentioned. This weevil may be avoided, it is said, by regularly changing the water once a week from the thirtieth day of the flow onward. In this operation the flood gates of ingress and egress should be opened simultaneously, so that the water may ebb and flow again with the recurring tide, or, where there is no tide, so that the water may be replaced as fast as it flows out, the level being maintained. Care must be taken in either case that no violent rents disturb the plants.

The "long point flow" is now succeeded by the period of dry growth. At the end of the sixty or sixty-five days, above mentioned, the water is drawn off, and the rice will be found to have attained a vigorous growth and to have tillered well, the plant being some 3 feet in height. The field should also be free from grass if the irrigation has been well conducted, though there is always more or less "volunteer" rice between the drills. The ditches should be flushed and cleaned out and the land allowed to dry, which will occupy about a week or ten days. The plant is now recovering from the effects of the "long point flow," which, though necessary, has somewhat weakened it, and is putting forth new roots and new leaves in its second growth. The beds should be kept dry, and no heavy hoeing should be done unless required by the presence of grass. "Volunteer" rice should be carefully pulled up by the roots and removed. A light hoeing is sometimes beneficial in order to admit air into the soil and to loosen it so that the new roots may easily penetrate it; such a hoeing should be very light, however, and small hoes should be used. In from fifteen to twenty days the roots have grown so as to meet midway between the drills, and the plant is beginning to joint. It must be carefully treated as a joint once broken can not be replaced. A last hoeing is now given and the "harvest" or "lay by" flow follows, about ninety days after the sowing of the seed.

In this final flow the water is let in to the same depth as that of the last of the "long point flow," and is gradually increased in depth after the plant has headed, but is never allowed to rise above the fork of the plant. The water should be changed every week by complete draining of the field and immediate flooding again, or where the fields are situated upon tidal rivers, by draining the field at low tide and filling it as soon as the tide returns. Some planters increase the depth of the water in proportion as the plant grows higher, and others prefer to have this "lay by" flow a shallow one, thinking that if too deep it encourages the presence of the weevil or other harmful insects. This flow lasts from sixty to seventy days, and only ceases a few days before the harvest.

Accounts differ as to the number, duration, and nomenclature of these various floodings. Many planters flood their crops four times; at first just enough to cover the seed until it germinates, calling this the "sprout flow" or "point flow." The water is then drawn off, and when the plants are 6 or 8 inches high the second flow commences. This seems to be indiscriminately called the "point flow" or "stretch flow," since it stretches up the young plants, causing them to grow upright, and lasts from twenty-eight to thirty-five days, or until the plants will shade the soil between the rows. This is then drawn off and a first and second hoeing given to the field. Then comes the "long flow," followed by the period of dry growth, and lastly, after a third hoeing, the "harvest flow," when the plants are about 18 inches high, which is kept on until the heads form and are nearly ripe. The soil is then dried for from five to ten days, and the harvest commences.

The rice plant after becoming fairly rooted is a hardy one, and the rough grain is not easily injured, but when in flower, which period occurs during the "harvest flow," the danger of injury is greater, since the blossom is very frail and easily affected by rain or by rough weather. A stormy August invariably diminishes the amount of the crop. A system of fallows and rotation has been practiced upon the South Carolina rice fields since 1837, though these fields hardly need much rotation, since rice does not greatly exhaust the soil and the soil is, moreover, yearly enriched by alluvial deposits from the water used, and, indeed, is ill adapted to any other crop. Manuring with rice straw, rice chaff, flour, etc., is also practiced, the necessary elements being thus returned directly to the soil. The fine qualities of long-grained rice are said to be mainly due to such manuring.

The "volunteer rice" or "red rice," above mentioned, is the product of the seed of the previous year's crop which has been dropped upon the field during harvest time, and, remaining in the soil all winter, has sprouted with the regularly planted crop in the springtime, growing with it and sharing its cultivation. Experience has shown that the seed which has thus "volunteered" or become self-planted produces a grain of inferior quality, this deterioration becoming more pronounced in each succeeding generation and being marked by a correspondingly increasing red color of the inner pellicle of the grain. If harvested with the crop this "red rice" would constitute a depreciation, and so must be carefully removed during cultivation. Its occurence may be in a great measure avoided, as follows: The harvest being gathered, the field is flooded to a slight depth for two or three days and the water is then drawn off, this operation being repeated once in two weeks until cold weather sets in; thus the "volunteer" seed is germinated and begins to sprout and grow, and is killed by the early frosts. It is important in selecting seed that it should be free from this "red rice."

HARVESTING.

The heads of the rice being well filled and all but the lower grains being hard, the time for reaping has arrived, and no time should be lost in doing so, as, it allowed to overripen, the grain "sheds" or "shatters," i. e., falls from the head with extreme facility, and is thus in a great measure lost. The "harvest flow" may be drawn off from the fields three to five days before the time for reaping, so that the ground may be in good condition for the operation. Reaping is best done with the sickle, though in some parts of Louisiana the "header" is said to have been used with success. The height of the plant varies between 4 and 6 feet. The rice is cut at from 12 to 18 inches from the ground, and the cut grain is laid upon the stubble in order to keep it off of the wet soil and to allow the air to circulate about it. After a day's curing the grain is removed from the field to undergo further operations, care being taken not to bind it while it is wet with dew or rain.

CULTIVATION OF UPLAND RICE.

This is more simple than that of lowland rice, and requires less preliminary outlay. Any soil is suitable for upland rice that is suitable for cotton, but it prospers best upon a level sandy soil inclined to be moist, and it is said, upon such a soil, to yield 3 bushels of grain where Indian corn upon the same field yields but 1 bushel. Preparation for planting may be made in the same way as for cotton, by plowing about 6 inches deep, thoroughly breaking up the soil with the harrow, and laying out in ridges. The drill furrows are made about 2 inches deep, and in these the seed is sown and covered over. It is important that cultivation should begin as early as possible in order to avoid grass, the worst enemy which rice has. The crop should be frequently hoed and a cultivator should be used. Reaping should be done as soon as the rice is sufficiently ripe, to avoid loss by "shedding." The crop generally matures in from five to six months after sowing, i. e., if sown about the middle of April it will be ready for cutting about the 1st of October. "White rice" is said to bear upland cultivation better than "gold seed."

CURING.

The harvested rice, after a day's curing in the field, is taken to the granary yards and there stacked in ricks. A common size for one of these ricks is 20 to 30 feet in length by 10 feet in height and 7 or 8 feet in width. Here the rice undergoes a heating process, due to natural fermentation, this heat being supposed to aid in maturing and hardening the grain. If, however, the process be not very carefully watched the heat is apt to rise too high and injure the grain, which is said to be "mow-burned;" and yet, if such injury be avoided the greatest heat that can be thus given is desirable. A rough method of measuring the temperature of the rick is by inserting a stake into the mass at either end. These stakes are examined daily by being drawn out suddenly, and if the inner point is found to be too hot to hold in the hand the rick must be pulled down, aired, and built up afresh; but if the stake is not too hot to hold, the rick must be left undisturbed. As soon as the heat is over the grain is ready for thrashing.

THRASHING.

This is done as for wheat and other grains. The hand-flail is now superseded by steam-thrashers provided with toothed cylinders and revolving rakes. The grain is screened in the same manner as wheat, and is then ready to be sent to the mills or to be shipped as "paddy" or "rough rice." The process of milling is hereafter described. The refuse from the thrashing is valuable as a fertilizer for the next crop.

YIELD AND PROFIT.

Good South Carolina rice lands will, when properly managed, yield from 40 to 50 bushels of "rough rice" per acre, valued at about $1 per bushel. The commercial standard weight of "rough rice" is 45 pounds to the bushel, and at this rate the above yield would be from 1,800 to 2,250 pounds to the acre. The cost of cultivation has been calculated at from $20 to $35 per acre.

GEORGIA.

In this State the cultivation of rice upon the tide-water lands is carried on in much the same manner and under the same conditions as in South Carolina. Before the late war the industry was a very flourishing one, and after the war it was revived and began to prosper; but within the last ten years it has declined, owing, it is said, to the dislike of negro laborers to the work among the marshes. Hence, the cultivation of lowland rice upon the marshes is being replaced by upland cultivation, which bids fair to become disseminated through the State and to make rice a staple crop. In the publications of the Georgia State Department of Agriculture (vol. VI, 1880), an account is given of a planter who produced over 100 bushels of rice per acre upon a creek bottom by means of irrigation, 20 acres being prepared and so arranged as to be flooded at pleasure. The seed was sown broadcast, the land flooded to cause germination, and the water then drawn off. The plants being well rooted, the water was again turned on and allowed to remain until a day or two before the harvest, the "dry growth" period of cultivation, as practiced in South Carolina, being omitted. By sowing broadcast there were many more plants per acre than if the seed had been sown in drills, and the labor required was small, the continuous flooding obviating the necessity for cultivation. It is not stated, however, whether or not such a mode of proceeding encouraged the presence of the water weevil.

LOUISIANA.

Before the late war rice cultivation was not very extensively carried on in this State, the main agricultural interest being that of the sugar plantations. What little there was was principally confined to the parish of Plaquemines, where the Mississippi flows into the Gulf of Mexico. The abandonment and destruction of the sugar plantations consequent upon the war offered, after peace was declared and agriculture resumed, an opportunity for rice cultivation upon a large scale, as a means of utilizing the old sugar fields. An impetus thus given, great strides were made and to-day fully one-half the rice crop of the United States is grown in Louisiana, and in many localities rice is said to be a more profitable crop than sugar ever was. The rice fields are situated in the above-named parish and among the low, swampy lands along the Gulf coast westward of the Mississippi.

Rice cultivation has some peculiarities in Louisiana, the main points of which are as follows: In this semitropical climate and upon the fertile soil of these lowlands grasses of many kinds flourish with extreme luxuriance and germinate as early as February and until June or July, and as grass of any sort is particularly deleterious to rice-growing, the planters are seriously inconvenienced by their efforts to get rid of it. When, after the war, the industry was first started it became customary for a planter to lease an old sugar plantation, generally for a term of three years, free it thoroughly from grass, cultivate his rice crop each year, and at the expiration of the lease abandon his land and hire a new plantation, recommencing the process. It was found that in about three years the grasses would make such headway that rice-growing became well-nigh impossible, especially as the water cultivation necessary for rice was exactly that best calculated to make the obnoxious grasses thrive, and even to increase, since grass seed was constantly being brought to the fields by the water used for irrigation. Finally, however, the supply of fresh land became exhausted, and attention was turned to methods by which the grasses might be kept down, so that rice fields already once used and abandoned might be reclaimed. It is hardly possible to do this completely, though one or two methods have proved successful in destroying the grass to a large extent, such as mowing after harvest and burning the hay as it lies on the field, or by burning off the grass after it has been killed by ice in the winter, but until some really effectual method can be found it will be difficult to establish permanent rice fields.

The method of planting followed in Louisiana is to sow broadcast at the rate of from 1 to 3 bushels of seed per acre, the best gold seed being used, the land being well prepared, and the planting done from March to June. The seed is harrowed in and flooding is commenced. This is differently performed by different planters, some preferring to flood immediately, letting the water barely cover the ground and drawing it off again as soon as the first signs of germination are perceptible. Others let the seed germinate without water, while others even germinate it before sowing, by soaking it in bags placed in the ponds, as is practiced in Japan, and then sow it broadcast upon the field, already covered by a shallow layer of water, and harrow under water. Whichever of these methods is followed, the rice is flooded when it has grown 3 or 4 inches high, the water not quite coming up to the top of the plant. The fields are kept flooded until just before harvesting, when they are drained in order to give the stalk strength, and to dry the ground for the reapers.

Upland rice succeeds well in Louisiana, as it seems to everywhere in the rice-growing States, though as yet its cultivation is not extensive, but is increasing. It is sown in rows or drills and cultivated with the hoe.

ALABAMA.

The marsh lands near Mobile are well adapted to rice cultivation, having a rich soil and being conveniently situated for draining or flooding. The process of cultivation upon these marshes does not materially differ from that used in Louisiana.

Following is an abridged account of experimental planting upon uplands in this State in 1871. In one experiment the soil was a sandy loam, free from gravel, and having a gray clay subsoil 8 to 15 inches below the surface, the fields being situated about 4 miles inland from the Gulf. Owing to the bad condition of the land, which was full of roots, etc., it was found necessary to place the drills about 4 feet apart, instead of from 15 to 18 inches only, as would have been done upon a sufficiently friable soil. The ordinary process of upland cultivation was used, and the harvest amounted to over 4 barrels of good rough rice per acre, valued at $20 per barrel. The yield of straw per acre was over 1 ton, valued at about $25, so that the total yield per acre exceeded $105. A second experiment was tried upon about three-fourths of an acre of well-drained upland soil, at high elevation. This land had been cleared two years previously, but had never been cultivated. The seed was sown in April, in drills 16 inches apart, and at first the crop was unfavorably affected by drought, but recuperated later on, being benefited by the July showers, and in October yielded a crop equivalent to 15 barrels of good rough rice to the acre, which was valued at $17 per barrel, together with 4 tons of straw per acre, valued as a forage at $25 per ton, making a total yield of $355 per acre. A final experiment was as follows: In February, 1871, an old field of 6 acres, which had lain fallow for ten years, was thoroughly plowed, and upon March 20 was planted with cotton. In mid-April this cotton was destroyed by insects and the field was then replowed and replanted with gold-seed rice, in drills 18 inches apart, and was carefully hoed at intervals. In the latter part of September the crop was harvested, yielding 171 bushels of rough rice per acre, valued at $1.15 per bushel, making a total of $196.65 per acre, the net profit being $24.86 per acre, exclusive of the straw, which was not taken into account. These figures show that upland rice can be profitably cultivated in Alabama, and that rice should eventually become an important crop in that State.

Upland rice is grown in Mississippi in the interior of the State among the pine regions, and is said to yield heavy crops. Lowland rice is also grown to some extent along the Gulf.

Rice succeeds fairly well in Texas, though its cultivation in that State can never compete with that of cotton. The area cultivated is situated along the coast and is very small, having been but 335 acres in 1879, the total crop being but 62,152 pounds of rough rice.

Finally, upland rice is cultivated in Illinois and in other States north of the thirty-sixth parallel. It is said to grow in arid soils and may be sown broadcast upon clean land in April, ripening in September. Crops have been gathered averaging from 25 to 30 bushels of rough rice per acre. It is probable that upland rice would succeed well in some of the Middle Atlantic States, as Maryland, Delaware, or New Jersey. It also might be more extensively grown upon the wheat lands of the North-west.

PREPARATION OF RICE FOR THE MARKET.

After thrashing, which is generally the last operation which rice undergoes upon the plantation, the grain is still in its husk, as paddy or rough rice, having an average weight of 45 pounds to the bushel, and in this form much of it is placed upon the market, especially for exportation, to be cleaned at its destination. But in order to prepare it for home consumption, it must be cleaned, that is, not only the exterior husk, but the interior pellicle must be removed and the grain brought to the state of pearly whiteness of thoroughly marketable rice. This requires two distinct operations and necessitates the use of machinery too costly to form part of the equipment of a plantation, so that it is rarely done upon the plantations themselves, as are the curing and thrashing, except in small lots by hand for immediate consumption. Indeed the industry of rice-cleaning is a separate one of itself, just as is the grinding of wheat to make flour in the Northern States, and thus rice-cleaning mills with husking stones and batteries of stamps have been established in South Carolina and other rice-producing States, as well as elsewhere in the country, the planters either sending their rice to be cleaned or selling their rough rice outright to the cleaners, who put it upon the market after they have operated upon it.

The first operation which the rice undergoes is the removal of the exterior husk. This is effected by passing the grain between burr-stones, by which the husk is literally ground off. These stones are generally about 5 feet in diameter and make 200 revolutions per minute. They are not grooved like ordinary millstones, since the object is not to crush the grain, but simply to crack and rub off the husk; therefore the faces of a pair of stones are made smooth and level and are nicely adjusted at a distance apart equal to the length of a grain of rice in its husk. A concavity in the center of the upper stone admits the grain, which, impelled by centrifugal force, revolves upon its shorter axis and passes between the stones, the husk being thus stripped off, while the kernel is left unbroken. Shorter grains escape unhusked. The rice is then winnowed to remove the husks, chaff, and dust, and is then submitted to a second operation to remove the inner pellicle, a thin, light colored epidermis adhering somewhat firmly to the kernel.

This is done by pounding the rice in mortars and does not differ in principle from the method in use all over the world, and practiced by the Chinese a thousand years ago. By pounding in mortars with heavy pestles each grain of rice is rubbed against its neighbors with force enough to rub off the pellicle, and if the force of the pounding be well regulated and be not kept up too long but a small portion of the grain is broken, while all the pellicles are removed. In this country the mortars are of wood or iron and the pestles are of wood, shod with iron, and weigh from 250 to 300 pounds each. A battery of these is arranged with canes very much after the fashion of a quartz mill in the gold-mining regions, and is driven by steam. The cost of a stamping mill of this sort has been estimated at about $1,000 per pestle, and a good mill for commercial rice cleaning averages about fifty pestles. The rice, having been sufficiently pounded, is then sifted and winnowed, and thus five products are obtained—chaff or pellicle, flour, fine broken rice, middlings, and, finally, whole, clean grain or "prime rice." The last undergoes a final operation of polishing and is then ready for the market. This polishing is done by passing the whole grains through a rapidly revolving screen provided with brushes or with wire gauze and sheepskins, whereby a brilliant surface is given to every grain.

By the tariff of March 3, 1883, the duty upon foreign rice in the United States was 2¼ cents per pound upon cleaned rice, 1½ cents upon rice husked but not cleaned, and 1¼ cents upon paddy. By the McKinley tariff of 1890, at present in force, these duties were reduced as follows: Cleaned rice is now admitted at 2 cents per pound, rice husked, but not cleaned, at 1¼ cents, and paddy at three-fourths of a cent. Thus there is a difference of 75 cents per 100 pounds between the duties upon cleaned rice and rice husked but not cleaned, so that the industry of cleaning rice now allows of a profit above the cost of cleaning. In San Francisco the consumption of rice is very large owing to the numbers of Chinese who inhabit that city, and the imports of foreign rice at that port amounted to 50,127,886 pounds in 1890. Thus the rice-cleaning industry flourishes at San Francisco, and there are several important mills there which clean rice by a new process with new machinery, the secret of which has not yet been made public, but it is claimed that by this process the rice is manipulated with very much less waste than by the old method of pounding. A new process, also kept secret or partly so, is in successful operation at Baltimore and it is claimed the machinery used can clean 35 bushels of rice per hour, and dispenses with the mortar and pestle. At Baltimore it is principally native rice which is cleaned.

WASTE.

In the process of cleaning rice by the burr stones and by subsequent pounding in mortars, about half the weight of the original paddy is lost, or, more properly, a bushel of paddy yields about half its weight, say 20 to 23 pounds, of clean whole grain rice, while the other half is not actually lost, as it may all be utilized either as broken rice, rice flour, or chaff, though of course the first are less valuable in their broken or ground up state than they would be in the shape of whole kernels. The broken rice and the flour are still valuable as food and are extensively sold as such. It is said, however, that by careful management, much of the breaking of the grain might be avoided and that a bushel of paddy weighing 45 pounds ought theoretically to yield from 30 to 35 pounds of clean, whole grain. The husks or chaff form about 20 per cent of the weight of paddy, an exact analysis of "gold seed" paddy showing—

	Per cent.
Husks	19.25
Grain	80.75
Total	100.00

the interior pellicle being neglected on account of its small weight. This would give 36 pounds of clean rice in a bushel of paddy, but practically so exact a yield is impossible, and there always must be some waste, even with the best machinery. The husks and the chaff and refuse from pounding may be utilized in either of two ways: they may be fed to live stock or they may be spread upon the soil as a fertilizer. The planter who sells his crop in the form of "rough rice" is in reality robbing his land of a valuable fertilizer, whereas he who husks and pounds his own rice loses some of the plant-food contained in the clean rice which he sells, yet the proportion thus lost is so small, and this loss is so overcompensated in the profit which the sale of his rice brings, that he does not feel it at all.

An analysis of the location of mineral matter in various parts of the rice plant, made by Prof. Shepard many years ago, will illustrate this. The mineral matter as a whole being reckoned at 100 per cent, we have:

	Per cent.
In the stubble and root	36.08
In the straw and leaves	36.08
In the husk	14.20
In the cotyledon and epidermis	11.70
In the clean rice	1.94
	100.00

The husk, cotyledon, epidermis, and the clean rice constitute the whole of the paddy. Therefore, calling the amount of mineral matter in the paddy 100 per cent, we have:

	Per cent.
In the husk	51.01
In the cotyledon and epidermis	42.03
In the clean rice	6.96
	100.00

Now, the planter who sells paddy retains and returns to the soil the 72.16 per cent of the total mineral matter of the plant which is contained in the stubble, root, straw, and leaves, while he loses the 27.84 per cent which is contained in the paddy, but the planter who sells clean rice loses only the 1.94 per cent contained in the clean rice, or say 2 per cent. Unfortunately for fertilization the 27.84 per cent must be lost, since the husking and pounding of the paddy upon the plantation can not be made to pay as far as large commercial crops are concerned, because of the cost of machinery, as has been above explained. There is a certain compensation, however, in the fertilization of rice swamps by alluvial deposit from the river every year.

The mineral matter of the plant finds its way back to the soil by various channels. The stubble and roots are plowed under at the fall plowing after harvest and have the whole winter in which to rot. The straw and leaves may be used as forage for live stock, and are thus converted into manure, or, if used as litter, they may be rotted in the manure heap. Even if burned their ashes are valuable. The husk and chaff, mixed as they usually are with a small proportion of broken rice and flour, make an excellent fodder for live stock, especially for swine, being richer in nitrogenous matter (gluten) and in saccharine matter than clean rice, and are thus returned to the soil under favorable circumstances as manure. The value of the plant as a fertilizer, however, depends more upon the quality than upon the amount of the mineral matters which it contains, and some parts are more valuable than others in this respect. Thus of the mineral constituents of the epidermis lost to the soil when the crop is sold as paddy, over 50 per cent consists of most valuable salts, while in those of the root, straw, and husk such salts do not amount to 10 per cent. Prof. Shepard goes on to say that the husk of the rice, which suffers conversion into humus with extreme slowness unless fermented with stable litter, seems to be overlooked by planters, and that as it contains over 30 per cent of carbon it must be capable, when incorporated with the soil, of performing to a considerable extent the functions of humus, that is, gradually giving rise to carbonic acid and of raising temperature by eremacausis. Besides this its minutely divided silica is in a more favorable condition for absorption by the roots of plants than that found in the soil itself. The husk also acts mechanically in opening the soil to air and moisture, but, unlike the stalk and leaf, it does not contain any alkali, so that perhaps the addition of wood ashes might be of benefit.

In the United States rice has but few diseases, and none of them have been thoroughly investigated by scientists. One or two smuts of rice are known but have not yet been written up. One of the commonest diseases of the plant is rust, which may generally be remedied by lowering the level of the water upon the fields. Another is a disease called by the Italians "*Brusone*," and which entirely destroys the crop; its causes and nature are more fully discussed under the account of rice-growing in Italy (page 70). In fact our agricultural literature is extremely poor in information upon this subject, which should form an interesting field for investigation.

On the contrary, the insect and bird enemies of rice are well known, and have been attentively studied and described. The following description of the more important insect enemies of the plant and of their work is condensed from the report of the entomologist of this Department for 1881, the observations having been made upon the rice fields of South Carolina and Georgia by Mr. L. O. Howard, principally upon the plantation of Col. John Screven upon the South Carolina side of the Savannah River, about 5 miles below the city of Savannah.

The water weevil (Lissorhoptrus simplex Say).—This is one of the principal of these insects, and is a beetle of the family of the *Curculionidæ.* For many years the rice planters of the Savannah and elsewhere along the Atlantic coast have been familiar with two insects, the one a minute white, legless grub, infesting the roots of the rice plant, and known as the "maggot," and the other a small gray beetle affecting the leaves of the plant, and called the "water weevil." It has now been ascertained that these two insects are one and the same, the maggot being the larva of the beetle. The adult insect makes its appearance in April and May, feeding upon the leaves of the young rice during the "stretch flow," and unless present in enormous numbers does not cause any very extensive damage. It generally feeds during the morning, and being semiaquatic in its habits and as much at home under the water as out of it, escapes the heat of midday by crawling down the stalk into the water below. The insect breeds at this season, the female laying her eggs among the roots of the plant.

After the "stretch flow" is drawn off the fields and the period of dry growth commences, the eggs seem to lie in a dormant state, only hatching after the "harvest flow" is put upon the fields, which is in July or August. Hence the popular idea that "the maggot is generated by stale water" during this flow. The presence of water seems necessary to the existence of the larva, and in practice the drawing off of the water for a day or two during the "harvest flow" affords a partial remedy and the maggot may sometimes be thus killed off, though generally the drying of the field sufficiently to do this effectually causes more injury to the crop than is done by the insect. The presence of this insect at the roots may be detected by the appearance of the plant, clumps here and there, or sometimes even whole patches, having a sickly, yellowish appearance, very different from that caused by the white blast described further on. The *Lissorhoptrus*, says Prof. Riley, is extremely common in all parts of the United States (east of the dry regions of the west) wherever there are swampy places, and may be found at all seasons of the year. It feeds upon a great variety of plants, mostly aquatic, such as the water lily, bulrush, sedge, and arrow head, besides upon wild and cultivated rice. Hence if the larvæ were effectually driven out from a rice field the field would soon become repopulated with them from other sources.

The rice grub (Chalepus trachypygus Burm.)—This is the larva of a large beetle of the family of the *Scarabæidæ*, closely related to the sugar-cane beetle and the sunflower beetle. This insect makes its appearance in May, at times when the rice fields are dry, and works its way into the ground, feeding upon the young roots of the rice and laying its eggs there. The larvæ hatch by June, and as long as the ground remains dry do much damage, but when the "harvest flow" occurs both the adult insects and the larvæ are drowned, since they are not of aquatic habits like the water weevil. Among upland rice fields where there is no irrigation this grub might do serious damage. This insect breeds among the dry lands at the back of the rice swamps where "volunteer" rice has been suffered to grow unchecked, and thence descends upon the cultivated fields. It is not known to attack any other plant than rice, and hence an easy remedy is suggested. The affected fields should be planted with some other crop for a year or two, while all the "volunteer" rice should be carefully removed.

The rice stalk borer.—This is the larva of a moth (*Chilo plejadellus* Trinck.) of the family of the *Crambidæ*, and is allied to the insect which attacks maize and sugar cane in a similar manner.

Mr. Howard, in the report of his observations at Savannah, writes as follows of this insect:

I noticed while passing through the fields that many of the rice heads were dead and white. I learned that this appearance was known as "white blast," and that the popular explanation of its cause was "poison of the soil." Such an explanation, however, would not account for the dying of one stalk in a bunch, as was almost invariably the case, so I immediately suspected insect work. I examined several of the blasted heads without finding any satisfactory cause, the head seeming dead from the base of the grain cluster, but below that point the stalk appearing sound. I soon, however, found a stalk where, at the first joint below the head, concealed by the sheath of the leaf, and inside the stalk, was working a very minute Lepidopterous larva, whitish in color, and striped longitudinally with subdorsal stripes of reddish brown. Soon after I found other larvæ of the same species lower down in the stalk, and at last reached a spot at the intersection of two ditches, where I found full-grown larva an inch long, quite at the base of the stalk, and also one or two healthy pupæ. In these cases the stalk appeared dead quite to the roots, all the leaves being brown and withered. In perhaps one-fifth of the stalks afflicted with the blast, this larva, either large or small, was found. I never found more than one full-grown individual in a stalk, but frequently found from one to six or eight young ones. All sections of the stalk seemed equally liable to be infested, the smaller larvæ being usually found nearer the head where the stalk is smaller, while the larger individuals from necessity were found lower down. The larva, as it increases in size, does not, however, continue to burrow down the center of the stalk to roomier quarters, as it might easily do, but apparently, when the stalk becomes too small for it at any one point, it bores its way out through a circular hole and crawls down the outside of the stalk to a lower point and enters again. The holes of exit and entrance are usually hidden, except at the very base of the stalk, by the clasping base of a leaf, the larva being obliged apparently to work its way into this tightly fitting crevice in order to get sufficient purchase to bore through the hard stalk.

There seems little enough for the larva to feed upon in the stalk, and it only eats the layer lining of the stalk cavity. When a larva is ready to transform (it is then at the base of the stalk) it continues its hole of entrance through the inclosing leaves, making it at the same time larger. It then returns to a higher position in the stalk (from 1 to 2 inches above the aperture) and transforms without reversing its position and with its head always from the opening. The duration of the pupa state is not more than five or six days. No observations have yet been made on the eggs, but they are probably laid on the upper leaves close to the stalk.

The adult moth is of a pale yellow color, with golden patches and scales, having as a rather distinctive mark a row of seven black dots at the end of each anterior wing. It seems to do no further damage to the rice plant after laying its eggs upon the leaves in order to produce the destructive borer, and in this respect differs from the water weevil, both the larva and the perfect insect of which feed upon the plant. There is apparently but one brood in a season upon the fields themselves, though a second brood is generally developed upon patches of volunteer rice beyond the fields later in the season. The stalk borer has an enemy of its own, which may serve in a measure to lessen its numbers. This is the larva of a small fly (*Phora aletiæ* Comstock), which may be found preying upon the pupæ inside the stalk. The best way to rid a plantation of the borer is to cut the stubble, "volunteer" rice, and weeds after harvest as close to the ground as possible, and then to burn them thoroughly in some safe place where the fire can not be communicated to the peaty tanks. The ravages of the stalk borer are somewhat limited upon the lowland swamps, and it would naturally do much more damage upon the upland fields.

White blast.—The exact nature of this effect upon rice is as yet but imperfectly understood. It may be caused by an insect, and it may be due to fungous disease or to other causes. It is discussed in substance as follows in the above-mentioned Entomological Report:[*]

According to the observations of Col. Screven, it is not unusual among the rice fields to observe here and there a few heads of rice, singly or in groups of from two to seven, which have an unhealthy, dead-white, gray, or "blasted" appearance. When this number of affected heads is not exceeded in a patch of 150 feet square the injury is pretty certain to be due to the attack of the above-described stalk borer; but when,

---

[*] Report of the Commissioner of Agriculture for 1881 and 1882: Report of the Entomologist, "Insects affecting the rice plant" (pp. 127–138).

as is sometimes the case, the injury is widespread and many heads are affected, the presence of white blast may be suspected. At first it was supposed that this disease was due to the presence of deleterious elements in the soil, popularly called "poison of the soil," aggravated, perhaps, by insect attack; but it was soon seen that this could not be the case, as all the rice was not affected alike, and as healthy plants could be seen growing upon suspected spots, and even a healthy and a diseased head could be found growing from the same root, and having originated from the same individual seed. It was also thought that a brackish condition of the water from accidental admixture of sea water might be the cause, but this idea was refuted by the fact that of two fields equally brackish one was badly affected by the disease and the other hardly at all. Another surmise was that certain localities might be especially favorable to insects, but this was also disproved. The attack of insects upon the pollen of the flowers and the presence of fungus have also been suggested as causes. It was observed that this appearance of white blast occurred after the "harvest flow" had lain upon the soil for about forty days, and generally affected the first heads which shot out, subsequent heads being generally free from attack.

The appearance of a rice plant affected by white blast is very similar to that of one affected by the stalk borer at first sight, but upon closer inspection one or two points of difference may be noticed. In stalk-borer attack the head is of a dead-white color, becoming afterwards gray from exposure to the weather, while generally the whole stalk and leaves of the plant, at least above the point where the larva is at work, are withered and brown. In white-blast attack it is generally the head alone which is affected, the stalk and leaves remaining green, and to all appearances perfectly sound and healthy, while the head at first becomes yellowish and then dead white, the distal end of each grain having a brownish spot, while later on the whole head becomes black, possibly from the presence of a fungus, the growth of which is favored by the diseased state of the plant. Very different from this is the appearance of a plant poisoned by sea water: the head shoots out covered with black spots upon the husk, and there is no dead-white appearance at all, while the leaves are red at the ends, and are also covered with black spots, and the whole plant finally dries up, the grains turning black and the husks remaining empty.

In examining rice heads affected by white blast, Mr. Howard found several insects, namely, *Scymnus fratemus* Lec, a species of *Orchelimum*, a species of *Thrips*, and also the common chinch bug (*Blissus leucopterus*). It is possible that white blast is the after effect of some insect injury earlier in the season, although no traces of extensive work either upon stalks or heads was to be seen. It may be due to the puncture of some insect, possibly by the chinch bug, which arrests the nourishment of the head and predisposes it to the attack of fungous growth, though no fungus was detected other than the black spots upon the husk, which might have been the result rather than the cause of the disease. The work of the water weevil may also have some influence in causing the disease as an after effect.

Several other insects are found upon the rice fields. One of these is the common "grass worm" of the Southern States (*Laphygma frugiperda* Sm. and Abb.), the moth of which lays its eggs upon the stalks. The worms, when hatched, cut the plants badly, and, when in great numbers, eat them quite down to the ground during "dry growth." When water is upon the fields they may be easily destroyed by drowning when knocked off the plant. In August and September the fields are frequented by myriads of the "lubber grasshopper" (*Romalea microptera*), which, however, seems to do little or no damage.

The ricebird (*Dolichonyx oryzivorus*).—There are many species of birds which prey upon the rice plant, but this one does more injury than all the rest together: it is also known as the reed bird along the Chesapeake, and the bobolink in the Northern States. The habits and ravages of this bird are described in the report of the Ornithologist of the U. S. Department of Agriculture for 1886, from which the present account is condensed:

The cultivation of rice in the Southern States is crippled and made precarious by the biannual attacks of birds. The name of the ricebird is familiar in the North, but the magnitude of its depredations is hardly known outside of the rice-growing districts of the Southern States. Innumerable hosts of these birds visit the rice-fields at the time of planting in the spring, devouring the seed grain before the fields are flooded, and again at harvest time in the fall, when, if the maturing grain is "in the milk" they feed upon it to a ruinous extent. To prevent total destruction of the crop during these periods of invasion thousands of men and boys called "bird minders" are employed, hundreds of thousands of pounds of gunpowder are burned, and millions of birds are killed. Still the number of birds invading the rice fields each year seems in no way diminished, and the aggregate annual loss they occasion is about $2,000,000.

The use of firearms has continued for more than a century, but has proved an expensive and inefficient remedy. Hence it is clear that some other means, consistent with reasonable economy, must be devised for the relief of the enormous losses now sustained by rice-growers from the depredations of birds.

The annual consumption of rice in the United States is almost double the production (see Table IV, page 76, of this report), and in quality the imported rice is decidedly inferior to that grown in this country, and the price paid for it correspondingly lower. The duty, though lately decreased by the tariff of 1890, is still too large to allow the foreign cleaned rice to be sold at much profit in this country, although there is, as has been above stated, a profit in cleaning foreign rice, as at San Francisco.

If, therefore, the bird plague can be abolished or reduced to comparative harmlessness, it is evident that great benefit will accrue both to the producer and to the consumer; for, the home demand being greater than the home supply, the planter will profit by increased production and lessened expense, while the consumer will gain by securing an uniformly good quality of rice, of much higher nutritive value than the imported rice.

In reply to a circular issued by Dr. Merriam, the Ornithologist of the U. S. Department of Agriculture, requesting information about the ricebird and its depredations, numerous letters were received, extracts from which are here given.

Col. Screven writes from Savannah, Ga.:

The ricebird is strictly migratory. It appears on the Savannah River about the 10th or 15th of April, and remains, perhaps, until the 29th of May. It appears again about the 15th of August, when the early grain is hardened and is not so inviting to his appetite as when unripe and "in the milk." Therefore the planter seeks to seed his land and to have his young rice under the water before the spring flock arrives, and to have the grain ripened before the autumn flock returns. If his planting is not finished before the spring flock comes it must be delayed until late in May or early in June, when the birds have departed for the season. The planter also looks to the ripening and harvesting of such late crops when the fall ravages of the ricebird have either ceased or are much diminished. The practice of the "open trench" system of planting offers an especially tempting opportunity for the ricebird to pick up the seed.

Though these ravages may be thus somewhat avoided the fields do not entirely escape, and the ruinous invasion goes on. The "bird minders" endeavor to drive the birds off by discharges of blank cartridges, and sometimes use small shot, when incredible numbers of the birds are killed, but even such measures do not prevent great waste. The voracity of these birds seems so intense that fear is secondary to it, and they fly, when alarmed, from one portion of the field to another out of gunshot, and immediately settle down again. The preventives above mentioned are but palliative, are applied at great expense, and are without commensurate results, and, in short, no effort yet tried, consistent with reasonable economy, will drive the ricebirds from the fields or afford any well-founded promise of their reduction to harmless numbers.

The bobolink.—Capt. William M. Hazard, of Annandale, S. C., writes in substance as follows:

The bobolinks make their appearance during the latter part of April. At that season they wear their Northern plumage, white and black, and sing merrily when at rest. Their flight is always at night. The bird minders keep up an incessant warfare, to prevent their pulling up the young rice, until about the 25th of May, when the birds suddenly disappear. They next appear as the ricebirds, in a dark-yellow plumage, and at this season have no song. Except when prevented by stormy south or southwest winds, they come almost punctually upon the 21st of August and the three following nights, settling upon the fields by millions, and apparently never flying in the daytime. They stay upon the fields until about the 25th of September, during which period every effort is made to save the crop. The loss of rice seldom amounts to less than 5 bushels per acre, and if from any cause there is a check to the crop during its growth which prevents the grain from becoming hard, the destruction of such fields is complete, it not paying to cut and bring the rice out of the field. Our present mode of trying to keep the pests off our crops is expensive, imperfect, and thoroughly unsatisfactory, yet it is the best we can do. The loss by birds and the expense of bird minders renders the cultivation of rice a dangerous speculation. One hundred bird minders will use from three to five kegs of gunpowder, weighing 25 pounds each, daily.

Mr. Theo. S. Wilkinson, a planter upon the Louisiana coast, writes:

The rice crop in Louisiana, from the time the rice is in the milk till harvest time and during harvesting, is much damaged by birds, principally the red-shouldered blackbird. Shooting is the only remedy thus far resorted to which is at all effectual, and it is only partially so. I have known rice crops to be destroyed to the extent of over 50 per cent, which is a loss of, say, $13 per acre. While this is an extreme case, a damage and expense of from $5 to $10 per acre is very common.

The red-shouldered blackbird (*Agelaius phœniceus*) comes next in importance after the rice bird as an enemy to rice, but though he does much harm he does at least some good by his destruction of insects.

The large boat-tailed graple (*Quiscalus major*), called "jackdaw" by the planters, also does much damage.*

The English sparrow.—In addition to his general destruction of our grain crops all over the country, and to his devastation among our fruit and shade trees, and to his persecution of our harmless native birds, the English sparrow (*Passer domesticus*), arch-enemy, it would seem, of all American agriculture, threatens to be almost as destructive to the rice fields in some localities as the rice bird himself, as he mingles with the latter, attacking the crops at the same time, and even attacks

---

* Report of the Commissioner of Agriculture, 1886. Report of the Ornithologist and Mammalogist, "Ravages of Rice Birds," (pp. 246–249).

the harvested rice in the stacks which the rice bird spares. Dr. Merriam says, in his Bulletin upon the English sparrow, 1889, p. 70:

The habit of working around the edges of a field seems to be characteristic of the sparrow, and is mentioned in scores of reports. Blackbirds, rice birds, and others which damage grain, are more apt to avoid the edges of the fields and settle in the midst of the grain where they are less likely to be disturbed, but the sparrow scorns to seek safety in the same way, but feeds unmolested wherever he chooses.

Again, page 76. he says:

Wherever the sparrow has reached the rice-growing districts he has damaged the rice to a greater or less extent, but this crop annually suffers so severely from the attack of rice birds and blackbirds that the presence of a few English sparrows is often overlooked. In the Middle States the rice bird feeds largely on the so-called wild rice, and often the sparrow may be found feeding in the same places.

Dr. Merriam also says:

The losses occasioned to rice-growers by the depredations of migratory birds are so heavy already that many planters have preferred to abandon the culture of rice rather than keep up the expensive warfare which is necessary in order to save any large proportion of the crop. By early planting it is sometimes possible to harvest a part of the crop before the rice birds arrive from the North, but should the English sparrow once obtain a strong foothold in the rice districts, and increase as rapidly as he has done elsewhere, the rice-grower will be compelled to fight a species which is present the entire year, which multiplies more than twice as rapidly as any native bird, and which is so ravenous and at the same time so cunning that it can not be combated successfully with the same means employed against the native birds.

Thus the rice crop is beset by enemies upon every hand, and at all times, from its earliest planting until the harvest or after. The rice bird, the water weevil, the stalk borer, the white blast, and again the rice bird, aided by the English sparrow, succeed each other throughout the season and descend in turn upon the fields. each doing its share of damage, in addition to the accidents of unfavorable weather, storm, floods, and salt water, so that the planter has more than the ordinary trials of the agriculturist to contend with, and is to be indeed congratulated should he brave them all and successfully conduct his crop to a profitable harvest.

RICE IN FOREIGN COUNTRIES.

ASIA.

CHINA.

This is probably the largest rice-producing country of the world, and the one which contains more land than any other suitable for its cultivation, but unfortunately no reliable statistics can be obtained, so that no estimate of area or production can be formed. Rice cultivation extends all over the southern and eastern portions of the Empire, as far north as the Yellow River, in 34° north latitude, and into the interior, prospering best among the lowlands about Canton and Kwangsi. Both lowland and upland rice are cultivated, but notwithstanding the vast area under cultivation the products fall far short of the home demand, and rice is imported from Siam and the Malay Islands if necessary. The exportation of rice from China has been forbidden by Imperial decree for several centuries.

Generally the rice lands are in the hands of large proprietors who lease them out to the farmers. The Chinese are rather gardeners than farmers, and the rice fields are usually divided into small lots of not more than three or four " mao "* each, that is, of from half to two-thirds of an acre, and often much less, though in certain localities holdings of from 100 to 150 mao (from 16⅔ to 25 acres) are common. The rent is at the rate of from $7 to $10 per acre per annum, and payment is usually taken in kind, the landowner taking about a fifth of the crop, though in some districts a full half often falls to his share. The landowner in some cases furnishes the tools and fertilizers, while the farmer finds the labor, an ox for plowing, and the seed, and cultivates and gathers the whole crop. Laborers can be hired for from $8 to $12 per annum. The instruments used are, as they have been for a thousand years, of the most primitive description and modern instruments and machinery are unknown as Chinese conservatism and distrust of anything foreign have always prevented their introduction. The hoe is the implement most frequently in use besides the spade and plow, the latter of wood shod with iron, such as we are familiar with only in museums and only serving to scratch the soil to a depth of 3 or 4 inches.

Inferior tillage, caused by these primitive instruments, is probably the reason why the soil of these rice fields, although naturally rich, needs a large amount of fertilization, and certainly the Chinese farmer places great faith in fertilizers and uses them unsparingly. The manure of horses and cattle is carefully collected, and a certain kind of oil cake is used. but the most esteemed fertilizer is the night soil from cities and large towns, which is constantly being carried to the neighborhood of the rice fields, where large tanks are constructed for its reception. in which it is allowed to undergo fermentation.

China abounds in rivers and in small streams. and has numerous canals from which water may be taken for irrigation. though there is no regularly organized system of irrigation works such as has existed for centuries in Japan. In localities remote from a natural water supply the farmers unite and establish reservoirs or wells for use in common. the water being conveyed to the fields by water wheels through a system of bamboo pipes. Upon hillsides and slopes the land is terraced so that the fields may be level, and these are so arranged that when the water is at a sufficient depth for the needs of the crop upon the highest level it will flow upon the next below. and from this to the third. and finally to the lowest level.

The system of cultivation of lowland rice in China, Japan. and India,

* A " mao " is about one-eighth of an acre, or 7,260 square feet.

and, in fact, throughout Asia, presents one important difference from the mode of cultivation practiced in the United States, namely, in the transplanting of the young plant when it is from 6 to 8 inches high, *i. e.*, when it is from fifteen to thirty days old. The different steps in the process of cultivation in China are as follows, and do not generally vary throughout the country, except in a few minor details:

A patch of ground, proportionate to the size of the field where the crop is to be finally grown and harvested, is liberally manured and is then broken up by the plow or spade, the manure being thoroughly incorporated with the soil and the whole being finely pulverized and made smooth, the rake being used for smaller and the harrow for larger patches. This operation takes place, according to latitude and the state of the season, from the middle of March to the middle of April. While this is being done the seed rice is also undergoing preparation, being placed in bags and soaked in water, running streams being preferred, until it commences to sprout, which is in three or four days. It is then sown broadcast and somewhat thickly upon the patch of ground prepared for it, and the water is let on to the depth of from 2 to 5 inches. The seed being already soaked will not readily float, and no attempt at covering it seems to be made. The water is kept upon the field until the young plant has attained a height of 6 or 8 inches, which will be in from fifteen to thirty days after sowing, according to circumstances of climate and weather.

In the meantime the fields for final cultivation are being prepared. The general method of doing this is to break up the soil with the plow or hoe and to turn on the water to a depth of 2 or 3 inches, letting it remain upon the field for a few days, after which it is drawn off and the soil is again broken up and thoroughly pulverized by the rake or harrow. Fertilizers are at the same time applied and well mixed in. In the province of Ningpo, this work commences about the 15th or 25th of April, at which time the rice fields are covered by a rank growth of wild clover. This is cut down and removed, and the soil dampened and well plowed. The cut clover is then thickly scattered over the field and plowed under, and the field is flooded and raked or harrowed under water until the whole surface is knee-deep in mud.*

As soon as the ground is ready and the young plants are sufficiently large the transplanting begins. The plants are carefully drawn from the bed, care being taken not to injure the roots, and are transplanted, two or three together, at about 6 inches apart, in rows 15 to 18 inches apart, this work often being done by women. Sometimes a second crop is set out, about three weeks later, between the rows of the first crop. The fields are then flooded to the depth of not more than 6 or 7 inches, this flow being sometimes continuous and sometimes intermittent in order to facilitate hoeing and weeding and lasting until about

---

* Consular Report No. 96, August, 1888 (p. 215).

a month before the grain ripens. Liquid manure is plentifully applied to the fields from time to time, and the crop is ready for harvesting in from three to five months after transplanting.

Upland rice is extensively grown in China, principally in the interior districts upon high lands requiring but little irrigation, and upon soils suitable for wheat or barley. Its cultivation requires much less labor and attention than that of lowland rice. The soil is plowed after thorough manuring and the seed is sown in drills, generally during March. The soil is kept loose between the drills and free from weeds, and liquid fertilizers are applied several times during the season. Harvesting occurs in September. Upland rice is said to have been introduced into China during the tenth century; there are three varieties of it, precocious, mid-season, and late-growing or Manchooria rice. It is generally considered to have a more agreeable taste than the lowland rice, but is less productive. In general all Asiatic rice is of smaller grain than that grown in South Carolina, and is not so white and is of less excellent quality. The best Chinese rice is said to be that produced upon the plains of Kiang-Su.

In Ningpo some fields were planted with poppy about March 1, the crop being gathered about June 1, and the ground then prepared and planted with a particular variety of rice, "*lo-mi*," especially grown for preparing a fermented liquor, "*samshu*," the crop being harvested in November. In many provinces, particularly where there are early harvests, two crops of rice are raised in a season, though very often the fields are planted with vegetables after the rice crop is gathered, not so much with a view to rotation as to utilize time and opportunity. Sometimes a crop of wheat or barley is followed by one of rice, not always the most profitable way of farming, but one in which the soil is not much exhausted and which saves expense for manure. The Chinese have long been accustomed to improve the quality of their rice by selection of seed; and a very old imperial edict, still in force, enjoins the selection of the largest seed for sowing.*

No improvement upon the ancient methods of harvesting and thrashing has ever been introduced into China. The grain is cut close to the ground with sickles, and is dried in the sun and afterwards thrashed by the flail or by treading out with oxen. The commonest mode of thrashing, however, is by beating the heads of the grain against the edges of a box into which the paddy falls. Winnowing is done by pouring the grain from baskets in the wind, large paper fans being used when the breeze is not strong enough to blow away the chaff.

Husking is done by means of stone rollers, and cleaning by pounding in mortars. These operations are not performed by the small farmers, who find it more profitable to sell their crops as paddy and to buy what rice they need for family consumption ready cleaned. Thus rice-cleaning forms a trade of itself, the rice-cleaners, who are

* Consular Report No. 102, February, 1889.

also dealers and speculators, sending agents into the country to buy paddy from the farmers. The husks are used in various ways, as for packing china, for mixing with building mortar as we use hair, or, finally, for fuel. The broken rice is ground into flour, and the straw is made into bags or hats or is used for thatch or as fodder for cattle. The idea of using the husks or straw as a fertilizer for the rice fields does not seem to have occurred to the Chinese.

The yield of lowland rice upon the best fields in China is said to average 5 piculs per "mao" when two crops are raised in a season, a picul being equivalent to 133⅓ pounds. This would amount to 4,000 pounds per acre, or 2,000 pounds at each crop, in the form of paddy. Upland rice is said to yield about 30 bushels of cleaned rice to an acre, weighing 60 pounds to the bushel, or 1,800 pounds of cleaned rice, equivalent to 3,200 pounds of paddy, since by the Chinese method a picul of paddy yields, it is said, 75 pounds of clean rice.

Rice is an important factor in the internal commerce of the Empire, even taxes being paid in it. A certain quantity of rice, generally of the upland variety, is sent to Pekin every year as imperial tribute for the use of the Emperor and his family and soldiers, and also for distribution in time of famine. This custom is of ancient origin, and is still kept up, though from many provinces an equivalent in money is now sent.

JAPAN.

Rice is the staple crop of Japan and forms the principal food of its people. It is cultivated almost all over the country south of 36° north latitude, wherever irrigation is possible, and flourishes best in the valleys, where the soil is very fertile. It is said that 95 per cent of the rice grown is lowland rice, though upland rice succeeds well and is attentively cultivated.

Very much the same conditions of rice cultivation exist in Japan as those existing in China. The land is divided in the same way into small lots, rarely more than an acre in extent, and often of not more than a fourth of an acre, so that the cultivation partakes somewhat of the nature of market-gardening. The same method of sowing broadcast upon a small field and transplanting to a larger is followed, and the crop is cultivated, harvested, and prepared for market in nearly the same way.

One or two differences, however, may be noticed. Although the rainfall in Japan is very heavy, varying from 60 inches annually upon the lowlands near the coast to 70 or 75 inches near the mountains or of 100 inches upon their slopes, irrigation is nevertheless an important factor in all Japanese agriculture, and has been successfully practiced for upwards of a thousand years. Large, costly, and solidly built irrigation works have been established throughout the islands, and mountain streams have been directed to supply them, the water often being brought from great distances by canals winding around the mountains, and thus the water supply is equalized throughout the year.

The implements used in Japan are fully as primitive as those used in China, the land being broken up by a wooden plow shod with iron and drawn by an ox or water buffalo, or even sometimes by a cow. Modern agricultural implements have not as yet been extensively introduced into the country, though American hand tools, such as hoes, rakes, or spades, would probably be appreciated, especially as the Japanese have not the same prejudice against foreign "barbarians" that the Chinese have. Improved and cheap rice-cleaning machinery might be more extensively introduced there, but the configuration of the land and the small size of the fields would render the introduction of reaping machines impracticable. The Japanese have one serviceable instrument peculiar to themselves. This is a mattock, or heavy hoe, with an iron blade about 16 inches long and 4 inches wide, and weighing some 6 or 8 pounds, the wooden handle of which is about 5 feet long. This instrument is, by a powerful blow, sunk to the full length of the blade into the soil, a large clod of which may be then turned by the leverage of the long handle. This process is a slow one, but seems to break up the soil in a manner that could not be done by the primitive plow above mentioned.

Like the Chinese, the Japanese pay great attention to fertilizers and use them plentifully. Night soil is carried from the cities and fermented in tanks and generally applied to the fields in a liquid state. Near the coast seaweed and fish are also used, and very often, as in the United States, rice straw, husks, and chaff are used, generally being rotted with animal manure. This economy of fertilizers has enabled the Japanese to raise, in some cases, three crops of rice in a season from the same land. Ashes of straw, grass, and bamboo leaves are also used.

Great attention is given to the selection of seed. The general method of doing this is to watch the rice as it matures, and when the stalk has assumed a perfect green color the time for selection has come. Close inspection will show that some parts of the rice head are of a very light yellow color, while other parts retain more of the color of the stalk, and it is these latter parts which are selected for seed, and are dried and stored with extreme care, being assiduously preserved from all dampness which would impair their vitality. Seed should not be selected upon low, boggy land, nor upon land of extreme fertility, the best seed being found upon a medium grade of soil.

As has been said, the Japanese method of cultivation is not essentially different from that practiced in China. The soil is prepared in March or April by flooding, manuring, and plowing, or breaking up with the mattock, and finally by leveling and harrowing. All soil removed in leveling is preserved to grow vegetables in. The seed is prepared by soaking in bags until it begins to germinate, or sometimes by burying the bags a foot or two deep in sandy soil. The seed bed having been prepared and reduced to a state of thick mud by flooding and harrowing, sowing is done from mid-April to May, the seed being sown broadcast, but not too thickly, at the rate of about 1½ bushels per acre. The young rice seems to grow more slowly than in China, as it is not transplanted until from six to eight weeks after sowing, and is then only from 4 to 6 inches in height. June 5 is a national holiday, or "transplanting day," and is a favorite date for performing this work. The beds upon which the young plants are set out are from 2 to 3 inches deep in water, and have been prepared in the same manner as the seed beds. Upon the best soils, well prepared, about thirty-six bunches, with from three to five sprouts in a bunch, are set out upon a surface 6 feet square, but upon poorer soils sixty-four bunches, with ten sprouts to a bunch, are set out in the same space. Care is taken to place the plants deep enough to obtain a good hold upon the soil, yet not too deep. After transplanting is done the field is flooded, and pulverized fertilizer, generally rape seed, oil cake, or fish scrap, scattered over the field and the water drawn off, leaving the soaked fertilizer about the roots of the plants. The field is frequently flooded during the growing season, but the flow does not seem to be continuous. The hoe is actively employed and all weeds are kept down. The Japanese also have a custom of pruning the roots of the rice, cutting off superfluous small roots which form on the tops of the larger ones. This requires a great deal of care and labor, no doubt, but it should be remembered that their fields are very small and receive all the attention of a garden. Even the eggs of insects are searched for and picked off by hand.

When the rice head begins to show, late in August or in September, a light yellowish tinge which foretells ripening, the water is drawn off and the field allowed to dry and the grain to ripen. Harvesting takes place early in October, the grain being cut with a sickle, and in favorable weather allowed to dry upon the fields. It is then bound in sheaves and carried to higher land to be thrashed at leisure.

Upland rice is grown upon the high lands, and in ordinary climates requires little or no irrigation. It seems to flourish as well in the northern parts of the main island, at about 40° north latitude, as it does in the central and southern portions. The dry soils are prepared with less than half the labor required for preparing lowland fields. In some favorably located districts the upland fields receive irrigation, but this is not the usual practice, and is seldom necessary. The seed is sown in April or May, from 1 to 1¼ bushels being used to the acre. Drills are made about 18 inches apart, and receive a compost of night soil, wood ashes, and well-rotted rice straw before the seed is planted, while during the growing season small quantities of liquid fertilizers are applied to the roots of the crop. Upland rice is never transplanted. The crop is harvested in September or October, the yield being less than that of lowland rice and the profits smaller in proportion. The lowland fields are allowed to rest during the winter, but after the rice crop is gathered the upland fields are often immediately replowed and manured and sown with wheat or barley.

Strictly speaking, rice is not thrashed in Japan, but is hatcheled or stripped, the heads being drawn through the teeth of a sort of rake made for the purpose. Winnowing is done as it is China. Husking is done by passing the grain between millstones formed of sections of bamboo. The grain is cleaned in the usual way by pounding in mortars, batteries of stamps being worked by water power where available. These operations are done at special mills, and not by farmers, who sometimes, however, husk their paddy by beating with flails upon straw mats. A small quantity of American rice-cleaning machinery has already been introduced at Nagasaki, and meets with approbation.

The straw and husks are utilized as in China, besides being used as a fertilizer.

The average yield of lowland rice is stated to be 50 bushels of paddy to the acre, averaging in weight about 53 pounds to the bushel, while that of upland rice is given as from 30 to 40 bushels to the acre. The best Japanese rice is said to be that grown about Nagasaki. This sells at from $2.40 to $2.80 per picul of 133⅓ pounds, and in quality is said to be second only to the best Carolina rice. It is understood that an agent of the Japanese Government is now in the United States to examine the South Carolina method of cultivation with a view to introducing it, as well as the Carolina rice itself, into Japan. It is to be hoped that the Japanese, as a progressive and intelligent people, will be more successful in this direction than have been the native planters in India.

The Government tax upon rice in Japan is very high, and often swallows up half the profits of the farmer. Formerly, as in China, the exportation of rice was forbidden, but several years ago this edict was repealed, and it is now hoped that production, previously regulated solely by home demand, will receive an impetus and that rice will become an important article of exportation.

INDIA.

In this country rice forms the principal food of 273,000,000 people, or of 18.6 per cent of the world's population, and is therefore the crop of greatest importance. The number of acres cultivated with rice reaches over 57,000,000 in an average year. It is produced in all sections of the country, upon almost every variety of soil, and under widely differing conditions of climate, altitude, and water supply, so that by continued and varying cultivation some 1,400 varieties of lowland and upland rice are now to be found there.

As in China, the rice lands are generally in the hands of native landowners (zemindars), who lease it out to the native small farmers (ryots) in small lots, the rent often being paid with part of the crop. The English inhabitants of India do not seem to take a prominent part in the cultivation as they do in that of indigo or of other crops, and the instruments used are still of a primitive character.

METHODS OF CULTIVATION.

The following accounts of methods of cultivation in different provinces are condensed from the consular reports and from a memorandum regarding the introduction of Carolina rice into India by Mr. L. Liotard, of the Indian agricultural department, Calcutta, 1880, who quotes largely from Dr. Balfour's "Cyclopedia of India."

In Bengal three principal varieties of rice are grown. The first of these is the "aous" rice, which is grown upon high, light, sandy soils, not subject to irrigation. It is sown late in April or early in May and grows during a part of the rainy season, which in the region of Calcutta commences in June and lasts until the middle of October. The crop is harvested late in August or early in September, requiring from three to four months for ripening. The second variety, known as "amun" rice, is sown upon low, alluvial tracts, and requires five months for ripening, being sown in June and July, during the rainy season, and harvested in November or December. In some parts of Bengal it is sown as late as the last of August, being gathered in the following January. This is usually the most profitable crop, though it is often seriously damaged by inundations, owing to unfavorable situation of the lands upon which it is grown. The third variety, or "boro" rice, is sown in January and reaped in May, and is common only in extensive marshy districts where it can be covered with sufficient water to protect it from too great heat of the sun. All these are varieties of lowland rice and transplanting is practiced when the young plants are from 8 to 15 inches high, a custom among the ryots being to place the plant in the soil with an inclination toward the direction whence the prevailing wind blows. Thus in Bengal much dependence is placed upon the rainfall, and a drought, which sometimes occurs, is usually followed by a failure of the rice crop, and sometimes by consequent famine. In some parts of this province there are canals for irrigation, but for some reason, not well understood, artificial irrigation in India, which is well conducted and to which attention has been given for centuries, does not succeed upon the rice fields, though it does so with other crops. The favorite rice among the natives of Bengal is what is called "cargo" rice, of large and sweet grain, but coarse and red. The Europeans prefer the "patna" rice, of smaller grain but very white.

In Madras rice is cultivated principally in the low-lying districts along the rivers, tanks being erected for a water supply. The soil is profusely irrigated at plowing time and converted into a soft mud, upon which the seed is sown, transplanting being performed upon part of the fields only, while upon others the crop is allowed to grow where it is planted. Water is kept on the fields until just before harvest, which in this latitude is not more than sixty days after sowing, as a rule. There are generally two crops in Madras, one being harvested in October and one in February or March, the latter producing the best grain. Owing to the expense of irrigation, rice is dearer in Madras than other cereals, so that the great mass of the people in the interior live upon other grains and pulse.

In Bombay, before the approach of the rains, the stubble of the previous crop, together with leaves, grass, etc., is burned upon the field, the ashes being allowed to remain as a fertilizer. As soon as the rains commence the ground is plowed to the depth of 3 or 4 inches, very often while the fields are inundated. In the meantime the seed is sown thickly in nurseries, and the young plants are transplanted when 4 or 5 inches high. About 100 pounds of seed to the acre are used for sowing, and the crop is gathered in from four and a half to five months, yielding, it is said, ninefold only, and often less. The following account of rice cultivation, from the Bombay Statistical Atlas, 1888, is quoted in Consular Report No. 128, May, 1891, by Consul Ballantine:

In the Konkan districts and in the moist areas with very heavy rainfall all along the eastern slopes of the Sahyádris, rice is grown continuously in lowlands, generally embanked to impound the rainwater. In these tracts irrigation is impossible, and the crop is solely dependent on the rainfall, which is entirely derived from the southwest monsoon. The rains burst suddenly and heavily, and are very continuous, but terminate early. These are the tracts where rice-seed beds are prepared by burning layers of cow dung or brushwood, with subordinate layers of leaves, grass, rice straw, and earth. The seed beds are on higher land than the fields into which the seedlings are transplanted, a necessary precaution to prevent flooding when the seedling is in its early stages. This is the ráb cultivation of rice, and has been declared by the forest commission, on adequate evidence from local inquiry and careful experimental cultivation, to be good farming and, under the peculiar conditions of the country where it is practiced, the best known method of cultivating rice. Other systems known and practiced are risky and incapable of extension beyond their present small areas in ráb tracts.

The peculiar circumstances referred to are: (1) The absence of heavy showers before June; (2) the very heavy rainfall; (3) the heavy continuousness of the early rain; (4) the early closures of the rains; (5) the absence of rain from the northwest monsoon; (6) the absence of facilities for water storage.

The other limited systems of growing rice in ráb tracts are: (1) The direct sowing of the seed in areas where the seedling is left to nature to harvest—a system only possible with the coarse variety of rice sown in lands on the seacoast either reclaimed from the sea or liable to partial immersion from the sea or tidal creeks, and thus largely impregnated with salt; (2) the raising of the seedlings in land heavily manured, either artificially or naturally. This system is of very limited application, and is only a means of preparing seedlings where ráb is not available or where ráb seedlings have been lost. It is risky and seldom remunerative, and its requirements limit its use to very insignificant areas.

The ráb cultivation of rice ceases in South Sarab at the River Lar, chiefly because rice ceases to be the most important staple and the manure is required for sugar cane and other more remunerative crops. Its cessation is not due to superiority of skill on the part of the cultivators, for ráb is fully utilized in Bassein and Mahin, in North Thána, where the cultivation is as skillful and admirable as in any tracts in the whole presidency.

Ráb again ceases on all sides where the peculiar conditions of ráb tracts are wanting. Thus in the Karnaták, outside the Mellad and to some extent within its limits, water-storage facilities exist. Here rice is drilled in terraced fields, with the advantage either of heavy showers in May, which enable the seed to be sown and to get a good start before the burst of the regular rains, or of irrigation water stored in tanks, by which the fields are flooded and the seed sown before the rains begin. This is the mode of cultivation in the rice tracts of Darwar and Belgaum. The variety of rice is different from that grown in ráb tracts. It is inferior, and has lost some of the characteristics of an aquatic plant. This is clear, because, if the early rain is not propitious, jowári, a dry-crop millet, can be grown instead of rice. Occasionally rice is seen on one terrace and jowári on the next, and even rice and jowári are sown in the same field. In Gujerat, where rice is grown in low-lying lands embanked as in the Konkan, the seed is raised in seed beds, manured but not rábed. This cultivation is possible, owing to local peculiarities of rainfall, even when irrigation is not available; but a large proportion of the rice in Gujerat is grown either under tank and well irrigation or as a pure dry crop. In the latter case it is drilled as in Darwar and Belgaum, but here (i. e. in Boroach chiefly) it is a row crop in cotton fields. It is thus almost a pure dry crop. This short account shows that rice, essentially an aquatic plant, is grown even as a dry crop. The extremes are met with in the row crop rice of Baroach and in the salt-marsh rice of the Konkan. In the latter case the seed is sown broadcast and left to grow where it falls. The seed is treated before sowing, to cause artificial germination. Where the land is very salt it is not touched till it has been inundated by the rain. It is then stirred with the bullock hoe and the sprouted seed is sown on the surface of the water. It falls to the bottom and takes root. It will stand complete immersion for ten days. Sometimes it is sown from boats. Where the land is less salt, it is carefully picked with the hand hoe in the hot season and left in the rough till the rain falls, when the sprouted seed is sown broadcast.

The artificial germination of the seed, which is not confined to salt rice, or even to rice, is caused in several ways.

There are very many varieties of rice, but it is sufficient for present purposes to show only how the varieties are influenced by the conditions of cultivation and rainfall as has been done.

One interesting method of cultivation most prevalent in Rutnagherry and Canara must be noticed. It is practiced with hot-weather rice, generally a late crop after the reaping of the monsoon crop. The field is kept flooded for a time, to kill weeds. The water is drained off, manure is applied, and the seed is sown in December. It is watered from time to time and ripens in March. The water is brought from a dammed-up stream or from a well or tank. This is called Vayangana rice.

Rice straw is not a nutritious fodder. The grain is easily separated from the ear by beating on a board or on sheet rock. The glumes are persistent, and clean rice is only separated by pounding with pestle and mortar. The cultivators usually sell rice in husk, and it is so kept by the ryots till a sale has been insured. The pounding is confined chiefly to large centers, of which Surat and Kalyan may be considered the most important. The straw is largely used for fodder, because where rice is a staple other fodder is scarce. It is also used as a thatching material and has the great property of keeping off white ants.

In Lower Sindh a very peculiar system of cultivation of rice is carried on upon the bhúlls. These are patches of alluvial deposit thrown up by the river Indus at its mouth, and consist of large tracts of swampy land thickly covered with mud and almost upon a level with the sea, so that they are alternately flooded with both fresh and salt water, streams of which intersect them in every direction. The rice fields depend for their cultivation upon this influx of salt water, and are surrounded by low dikes or bunds in order to regulate its flow as well as that of the fresh water. The rice grown upon them is a red variety of lowland rice of inferior quality. This singular method of cultivation is thus described by Dr. Balfour:

Should the river, during the high season, have thrown up a bhúll. the zemindar, selecting it for cultivation, first surrounds it with a low bund of mud, which is generally about 3 feet in height. These bhúlls, being formed during the inundation, are often considerably removed from the river branches during the low season. When the river has receded to its cold-weather level, and the bhúll is free of fresh water, he takes advantage of the first high spring tide, opens the bund, and allows the whole to be covered with the salt water. This is generally done in December. The sea water remains on the land for about nine weeks, or till the middle of February, which is the proper time for sowing the seed. The salt water is now let out, and as the ground can not, on account of the mud, be plowed, buffaloes are driven over every part of the field, and a few seeds of the rice thrown into every footmark, the men employed in sowing being obliged to crawl along the surface on their bellies with the basket of seed on their backs, for were they to assume an upright position they would inevitably be bogged in the deep swamps. The holes containing the seed are not covered up, but people are placed on the bunds to drive away birds until the young grain has well sprung up. The land is not manured, the stagnant salt water remaining on it being sufficient to renovate the soil. The rice seed is steeped in water, and then in dung and earth for three or four days, and is not sown until it begins to sprout. The farmer has now safely got over his sowing, and as the rice is not, as in other cases, transplanted, his next anxiety is to get a supply of fresh water, and for this he watches for the freshets which usually come down the river about the middle and end of February, and if the river then reaches his bhúll he opens his bund and fills the inclosure with the fresh water. The sooner he gets this supply the better, for the young rice will not grow in salt water and soon withers if left entirely dry. The welfare of the crop now depends entirely on the supply of fresh water. A very high inundation does not injure the bhúll cultivation, as here the water has free space to spread about. In fact the more fresh water the better. If, however, the river remains low in June, July, and August, and the southwest monsoon sets in heavily on the coast, the sea is frequently driven over the bhúlls and destroys the crops. It is, in fact, a continued struggle between the salt water and the fresh. When the river runs out strong and full the bhúlls prosper, and the sea is kept at a distance. On the other hand, the salt water obtains the supremacy when the river is low, and then the farmer suffers. Much bhúll crop is destroyed in the monsoons and during heavy gales. The rice is subject to attacks also of a small black sea crab, called by the natives *kookace*, and which, without any apparent object, cuts down the growing grain in large quantities and often occasions much loss. If all goes well, the crop ripens about the third week in September and is reaped in the water by men, either in boats or on large masses of straw rudely shaped like a boat, and which, being made very tight and close, will float for a considerable time. The rice is carried ashore to the high land, where it is dried and put through the usual harvest process of division, etc., and the bhúll is then, on the fall of the river again, ready for its annual inundation by sea water.

The above provinces are mainly upon the coast or in its neighborhood. In some of the inland provinces of India cultivation of rice is carried on as follows:

In the northwestern provinces and Oudh the rice succeeds best in a heavy soil with plenty of water. The best varieties are sown in beds, being afterwards transplanted at a distance of 5 inches apart. Thus, upon good soil, the plants grow to 5 or 6 feet in height and produce a large quantity of grain. Inferior varieties, of which there are many, are sown broadcast in June and left to ripen without transplanting.

In the Punjab, rice is grown in many of the plain districts, especially along the banks of the rivers. A celebrated upland variety, the Bara rice, is grown in the valley of Shaik Khan, near Peshawar, and is highly prized and is in great demand at Cabul. Scarcely less prized is the basmati rice, described as being of large, white, and fragrant grain, and grown in the Kangra Valley. Unfortunately, the methods of cultivation of these two varieties are not described.

Dr. Balfour thus describes cultivation in Kashmir:

Rice is sown in the beginning of May, and is fit to cut about the end of August. The grain is either sown broadcast in the place where it is intended to stand till it is ripe, or thickly in beds, from which it is transplanted when the blade is about a foot high. As soon as the season will admit after the 21st of March, the land is opened by one or more plowings, according to its strength, and the clods are broken down by blows with wooden mattocks, managed in general by women with great regularity and address, after which water is let in upon the soil, which, for the most part of a reddish clay or foxy earth, is converted into a smooth, soft mud. The seed grain, put into a sack of woven grass, is submerged in a running stream until it begins to sprout, which happens sooner or later according to the temperature of the water and of the atmosphere, but ordinarily takes place in three or four days. This precaution is adopted for the purpose of getting the young shoots as quickly as possible out of the way of a small snail which abounds in some of the watered lands of Kashmir, but this sometimes proves insufficient to defend it against the activity of this destructive enemy. When the farmer suspects by the scanty appearance of the plants above the water in which the grain has been sown and by the presence of the snail drawn up in the mud, that his hopes of a crop are likely to be disappointed, he repeats the sowing, throwing into the water some fresh leaves of the Praugos plant, which either poison the snails or cause them to descend out of the reach of its influence. The seed is for the most part thrown broadcast into about 4 or 5 inches of water, which depth is endeavored to be maintained. Differences of practice exist as to watering, but it seems generally agreed that rice can scarcely have too much, provided it be not submerged, except for a few days before it ripens, when a dried state is supposed to hasten and to perfect the maturity and improve the quality of the grain. In Kashmir it is customary to manure the rice lands, which is never done in Hindustan. This manure for the most part consists of rice straw rejected by the cattle and mixed with cow dung. It is conveyed from the homesteads to the fields by women in small wicker baskets, and is set on the land with more liberality than might have been expected from the distance it is carried. Many of the rice lands are situated much higher than might be thought convenient to Hindustan, and are rather pressed into this species of culture than naturally inviting it, but still they yield good crops through the facility with which water is brought upon them from the streams which fall down the face of the neighboring hills. In common seasons the return of grain is, on an average, from 30 to 40 for 1, besides the straw.

In Nepaul the Joomla rice is extensively grown. This is an upland variety, which, on account of its peculiarity of flourishing seemingly without inconvenience amid the snows and frosts of the Himalayas at an elevation of from 6,000 to 7,000 feet, botanists have named *Oryza nepalensis*. The method of planting is as follows: The seed is heaped in a cool place and covered with layers of moist earth and rich manure, and thus sprouts in from ten to twelve days. The ground is prepared for planting by being plentifully covered with water, and is then plowed into a thick mud and the seed is sown broadcast, growing where it falls until the harvest without transplanting, water being applied to the fields with discretion during growth.

Lower down upon the mountains, between 5,000 and 3,000 feet altitude, other varieties of upland rice are grown, including the "clammy" rice, *Oryza glutinosa*, already mentioned; no irrigation being necessary on account of the dampness of the summer months. Joomla rice is said to have been successfully raised as an experiment in England, the planting having been done upon the banks of the Thames, near Windsor.

THE INTRODUCTION OF CAROLINA RICE.

The reputation which our South Carolina rice has always enjoyed for its superior qualities of size of grain, whiteness, and superior yield, has caused the Indian Government to attempt its introduction into that country, and at the same time to study the methods of cultivation practiced in the United States in the hope that thus many native species might be improved, or at least replaced. Experiments were begun in 1868 and were continued for several years, and although a certain amount of success was obtained in certain of the provinces, no very definite conclusions as to the advisability of its introduction were reached. It is possible that further experiments may be made at some future time in this direction, since there is abundant room for improvement in the cultivation of Indian varieties. The experiments made were duly recorded, and an account of them has been given by Mr. Liotard in the memorandum above referred to, from which the following notes are taken:

Early in 1868 10 tons of Carolina rice seed (presumably the best Gold-seed rice, though this point is not stated) were obtained by the Indian secretary of state at London and were sent to India for distribution among the various provinces. This seed was packed in 200 barrels, holding 120 pounds each, a certain proportion of kiln-dried rice husks mixed in each barrel to preserve the rice.

Two previous attempts had been made to grow Carolina rice in India, and had been successful, or at least partially so. One of these was conducted by the government of the presidency of Madras and one by the Agricultural and Horticultural Society of India, both with seed privately obtained from Charleston. The Indian Government therefore secured a quantity of the seed of this rice, already acclimatized at Madras, and sent it to Bengal for trial along with the fresh seed from South Carolina. All the seed was given, in June, 1868, to such planters and zemindars as were willing to undertake its cultivation, and a general record of the experiments and their results is as follows:

The reports, besides pointing to the fact that the seed had been received too late for a fair trial, showed that its cultivation had been carried on without any uniform system. The results proved what might have been expected, namely, a long series of more or less complete failures. A few solitary instances, however, gave some promise of future success and some of the local authorities suggested a fresh trial.

Thus in Bengal, where it was said that many failures were due to the late arrival of the seed, the following experiments showed some success. At Dumdum, near Calcutta, equal quantities of Carolina and Madras acclimatized seed were sown side by side and cultivated under the same conditions. All the seed germinated freely. When about a foot high the young plants were transplanted, five or six in a bunch. The acclimatized seed produced nearly three times as large a crop as the Carolina, and it was afterwards found that the former had had an advantage of soil not suspected when the transplanting was made. Both varieties are said to have remained unaffected by bad weather in October, which beat down and destroyed native crops in neighboring fields. In another experiment at Calcutta there was much variation in yield, being from four to forty-eight times the quantity of seed sown, owing, doubtless, to want of care, but where great attention was given a fair yield was obtained and the people seemed pleased with the seed. In Palamow the seed was sown in a bed in July and transplanted to a loamy soil mixed with sand. The ear formed in October, ripened in November, and was out in December, the yield being eight for one, which is considered a fair yield. It was considered in every way superior to native rice; the plants were healthy, and though suffering a little from want of rain, did not suffer so much as the native crops. A comparison between the Carolina and the acclimatized rice showed that the latter had not apparently degenerated from acclimatization. It was said that the result of the experiment would have been more satisfactory had the sowing taken place in June instead of July, and that the Carolina seed appeared well adapted to the deep rice lands of the country.

In Oudh the seed also generally arrived too late, and the year 1868 was one of drought in many places. Modes of cultivation were not stated, and nearly all experiments were failures. In one locality, Goudah, it was said that the Carolina seed failed on account of the drought, though the native crop "was not so bad."

In the northwestern provinces the seed came too late and there was also drought, and no success was reported, which was looked for however in 1869. The same thing happened in the Punjab. Rice is not an article of general consumption among the poorer classes in the Punjab as it is in Bengal. Carolina rice can be grown there with due care, but rice cultivation in this province is not sufficiently important to render it likely that success will be attained in introducing a new variety, especially since the natives think it inferior.

In the central provinces the seed was received in good time, but the year is said to have proved unfavorable, owing to want of rain, and almost all trials failed. In Chanda, however, some of the seed gave twenty-two-fold upon land where native varieties gave but tenfold. Details of cultivation were not given. At Raipur the best results were obtained by Mr. Duncan Sinclair. A quantity of seed was sown June 11 and sprang up vigorously on the 15th, requiring no water until the 18th, after which it was watered five times, and was, on July 23, after a heavy shower, transplanted to ground containing a large proportion of black loam and prepared for the purpose. Two plants were put together, the pairs being 5 inches apart. No rain having fallen up to August 2 well water was given, and the plants wore a healthy appearance and took root. A heavy shower then fell and the plants made rapid progress. There was very little rain in September and October and irrigation was largely resorted to. The harvest amounted to thirty fold. This is stated to have been an extraordinary result, considering the state of the season, native seed in the same locality yielding, in good soil and with an average rainfall, from fifteen to twenty-five fold. Mr. Sinclair remarks of the Carolina seed that it threw forth a strong stem and as many as eleven offshoots, each of which produced an ear as long as that of the main stem. The rice was coarse, but had a good appearance after boiling. It had no scent, which was considered a great disqualification by the natives, who held the country rice as superior, yet nevertheless begged for Carolina seed.

In British Burmah, where rice succeeds better than in almost any part of Asia except Siam, and where there is an immense cultivation of it and much exportation, the experiments are reported to have been unsatisfactory, though it was observed that with proper care Carolina rice should grow well in that country. Good results, however, were obtained in Shweggeen and Amherst, forty-eight and fifty fold being harvested in the former district. The seed was sown broadcast, in July in Amherst and in August in Shweggeen, and the harvest in each case was gathered in three months after sowing, or a month earlier than the native Burmah crop. The straw was thicker and coarser, the ears longer and fuller and three times as heavy as those of the ordinary indigenous paddy. The root struck deeper in the ground, thereby offering more resistance to high winds and heavy rains. The seed was said to be unsuited (?) for cultivation in low inundated lands and to have thriven better on high land, where there were not more than 2 or 3 inches of water during the rains. The great tenaciousness, however, of the Carolina paddy to its husk, rendering thrashing (husking) difficult, was looked upon as a serious objection. Complaint was also made that it was "unfit for human consumption," since it was hard to boil and was not agglutinous. The objector, however, admitted that "the taste was good and it is more satisfying than our rice."

The Madras experiments seem to have been carried out more intelligently than in other provinces. In the garden of the jail at Chingleput, Dr. Thompson, the superintendent, made trials under varying con-

ditions. Equal quantities of seed were sown as a wet crop and as a dry
crop, and each of these two methods were further tried by both broadcast sowing and transplanting. The soil was a sandy clay a foot and
a half deep and was manured with surface silt. The subsoil was stones
and rubbish, the plot of ground being a disused ditch which had been
filled up and where two or three crops of hay had been mowed since
it was last tilled. For the wet cultivation the nursery and beds were
prepared in the native way, by trampling in leaves and twigs, and,
when these were well worked in, the seeds, which had been germinated
by soaking, were sown broadcast, August 10, into wet bed No. 1 and
also separately placed in a nursery for transplantation into wet bed
No. 2. In a month from the date of the sowing the plants were 2 feet
high with roots nearly 5 inches long, and those in the nursery were
transplanted into wet bed No. 2. The heat at this time was great, so
that the plants withered much and were thus thrown back two weeks,
but after recovery they grew rapidly, and when wet bed No. 1 was
reaped, which was on November 30, those in bed No. 2 were in full
ripe ears and nearly of the same height. They were cut fourteen days
after the broadcast crop and yielded 123 fold. The crops in these two
beds required comparatively little tillage, being simply watered daily
and protected from birds. They were greatly blown about by strong
winds and rain early in November, when the plants in the broadcast
bed No. 1, being heavy with ears, fell to the ground and suffered much
in consequence. The dry cultivation was also done by broadcast sowing and by transplanting. For this, two beds and a nursery were well
plowed, cleared of weeds, and leveled. On August 13 the nursery was
sown with dry seed and the earth again plowed, raked, and watered.
The plants were transplanted when thirty-eight days old, and although
seven days older at this time than the plants in the wet nursery were
when they were transplanted, yet they were not nearly so well grown
nor as healthy looking. Therefore the crop was converted into a wet
one. The effect was great, and the plants grew rapidly and became
healthy, tillered well, and, although much shorter than those in the wet
bed, yielded 121 fold when reaped on December 21. The broadcast
bed was not sown until August 31, and the plants were slow in growth,
being when a month old very little better in appearance and size than
native plants. On being converted into a wet crop, when about 2
months old, they grew rapidly and tillered even better than any of the
others. The amount of their yield is not stated.

Dr. Thompson was of the opinion that Carolina rice is easy of cultivation and can be cultivated in Madras at any season of the year when
water is at hand, and is, moreover, very hardy. As an experiment,
he found plants to grow after half or even all the roots had been cut
off and to bear ears as well as other plants not thus injured, thus
bearing out the fact that the order to which the cereals belong is
characterized by the tenacious vitality of its plants, as is seen in the

grasses. With regard to the water supply. it appears that the crop should be flooded during the first month. but should receive but little water during the second. Dr. Thompson gives preference to the broad-cast method of sowing. since by transplanting the plants did not tiller so well.

The Government report upon the above experiments stated that owing to the late receipt of seed and the unfavorable nature of the sea-son the experiments could hardly be considered to have had fair play, and that it was desirable to await the result of further trials there being made with acclimatized seed and with fresh seed from Carolina.

In the year 1869 experiments were continued with some of the seed received too late for sowing in 1868, and also with seed resulting from the experiments above related. There were many successes and many failures, which could admit of but one explanation: success was the result of experiments conducted intelligently and with good will, while failure resulted from the experimenters "simply throwing the rice away and reporting that that they had sown it and that it did not germinate," or else. as in Madras, where results were very good. the cultivators delib-erately made false reports in order to keep the produce all to themselves. In June. 1869. the following very short memorandum of the method of rice cultivation as practiced in South Carolina was distributed among the Indian rice-growers:

Rice is sown in long drills made by hoes (machinery does not work well) of about 1 foot deep; drills 1 foot apart; 2 bushels to an acre. Water is let on as soon as the rice is 3 inches high, and it is kept under water, that is, the water is kept to within 2 inches of the tops, until it (rice) is about 4 inches high; it is then drawn off and the weeds are taken out. After this the water is let on again; when it begins to head the water must be allowed to rise just below the head (that is the point where the kernels grow). The water must be high enough to keep the stem steady in case of wind.

Mr. Liotard notes several successful experiments in 1869, only one of which is of interest, as follows:

Mr. Sinclair, the settlement officer at Paipoor, in the Central Provinces, continu-ing his work of 1868, tried experiments in two fields in two different ways. One he cultivated somewhat after the above South Carolina method, the soil being a mid-dling clay, but not deep. The field had lain fallow several years. but had received silt from elevated lands about it. It was plowed once and liberally manured in June, was planted in July, weeded in August, and the crop was cut in November. The average height of the plant was 5 feet, with stalks one-fifth of an inch thick, each plant having twelve shoots on an average and each shoot an ear averaging 6 inches long. The second field was cultivated after a native method; it had a mixed clay and sand soil and a favorable water supply, and had lain fallow a year; it was not manured. as the rains overtook the preparation of the land. The seed was sown broadcast. and, on attaining the height of 1 foot, was treated after the "be-asna" method peculiar to the district. The field was bunded or diked and all escape of water prevented. On there being 6 inches of water in it a light plow was used and the plants partially uprooted and the water then allowed to drain off. so as to give the roots the benefit of the sun. The water, however, is not generally drained off unless the weather be cloudy and there be prospect of rain. After this the field is weeded and the harvest gathered. The height of the plant in this field was 3 feet and there were not more than six or seven shoots to a plant, with ears only about 5 inches long, and the straw was inferior. From these results Mr. Sinclair deduces the following rules for growing Carolina rice in the Central Provinces: (1) The soil must be of loose clay and sand mixed; (2) it requires manuring; (3) it must be clear of weeds when the plants are put down; (4) transplantation is the most satisfactory process; (5) the seed for transplantation must not be thrown in too thick, or the plants get long and weak and take a long time after transplantation to acquire vigor; (6) the plants must be put down 8 inches apart; (7) after transplanting there must not be too much water in the field; in fact, it must be kept as a mere puddle until the plants erect themselves, and then water may be let on or retained in the field sufficiently to cover all but 2 inches of the tufts; and, after the plants are 1 foot high and well in the soil, the more the better.

It is unfortunate that a fuller and more detailed account of Mr. Sinclair's experiments is not given.

For the experiments of 1870 fresh seed was obtained and left Charleston in perfect condition in December, 1869, being distributed among the provinces in May, 1870. On the whole, the experiments were more successful than in previous years, yet there were many failures, real or feigned, and in some cases these were due to want of system. In Bengal nineteen successful plantings are recorded by Mr. Liotard, which, however, show nothing of interest beyond the experiments already quoted except a few remarks such as the following:

This grain is most peculiarly liable to the attacks of beetles. * * * The Carolina rice suffered somewhat from blight, whereas the native did not. * * * One crop has been gathered and the stalk is throwing out a second crop, and a third crop, it is expected, will be reaped before the plants die out. * * * The Assamese grow their paddy with so little trouble and get such good crops that they will be slow to abandon its cultivation even to insure a more profitable return for their labor. * * * The chief advantage in Bengal is the presence of so many European gentlemen in the interior, but they do not cultivate rice or any other ordinary staple on a large scale, and only grow samples by way of experiment.

The Oudh experiments failed altogether. In the northwestern provinces the experiment proved a failure in nine districts, a partial success in seven, and a decided success in two. It was remarked that—

The absence of any scientific system or knowledge on the part of those who tried the experiment and the inability of district officers to supply this defect or to devote to the experiment the care and attention necessary to render the trial considered as one of the suitability of this rice to the northwestern provinces, generally barren of results.

In the Punjab successful results were obtained in two districts out of seven. It was remarked that—

No one who has tasted Carolina and Indian rice can hesitate in considering that the latter is far the most palatable; and it is not to be wondered at that the people consider the Carolina rice inferior to the produce of country seed, especially when it is remembered that rice cultivation has attracted the attention of the people in the Punjab for centuries and that a greater number of varieties of rice than of any other crop is known and commonly recognized.

On August 7, 1871, the Government of India published a review of the results thus far obtained, saying that, although the Government was not yet in a position to decide authoritatively as to the exact merits of the Carolina rice as compared with the several indigenous varieties and although the opinions of different officers and the reports of the results obtained in different localities were very discordant, there appeared to be generally a balance in favor of the superior utility of the American plant, the advantages of which might be summed up as follows:

(1) The Carolina paddy plant is more hardy, as it is less easily injured by gales and heavy rains, which entirely prostrate the Indian kinds. It requires a less amount of water than the Indian plant; it suffers less from drought and also (according to some authorities) from floods.

(2) The produce of this species of rice is much greater than that of the country kinds—(a) In respect of its yield in grain it gives a much larger gross weight of rice in the husk, and, the husk being thinner, it yields a larger proportion of clean rice to rice in husk, and, when ripe, it does not drop its seed in consequence of a little rain or wind, as the Indian varieties generally do; (b) the straw is longer and stronger than that of Indian rice, and can be utilized for thatching and other purposes for which the Indian straw is almost useless. In Burmah it is said to be greedily devoured by cattle.

(3) It ripens earlier and in a much shorter time than the indigenous varieties, so that in Burmah and in some places on the continent of India it would be possible to obtain two crops of Carolina for one of the common Indian rice.

(4) When properly attended to it appears to improve rather than to deteriorate by cultivation in India.

On the other hand the following are the disadvantages of the Carolina rice:

(1) Its quality (according, at any rate, to Indian ideas) is somewhat inferior. It has little flavor and scarcely any scent. It is believed to contain somewhat less nutriment,[*] is less liked by native consumers, and commands at present a lower price among them.

(2) The grain is much more difficult to.thrash out.

(3) The straw is coarser, and, in some localities, is said to be less liked by cattle.

In regard to this latter opinion a report from Madras in 1869 states: "It yields a larger amount of straw of a sort also more succulent and palatable than that of ordinary paddy." (The word "paddy" is used in India to designate the growing plant as well as the grain in the husk. It is derived from *pádi*, the Malay name of the rice plant.) In regard to the first of the above objections a report from Madras says: "The seed was sold for one anna a measure; the same price as for native seed, but afterward rose to two annas a measure."

Other reports from Bengal, Travancore, and Cochin were generally favorable to Carolina rice.

In conclusion [says Mr. Liotard], it may, in a few words, be asserted that Carolina paddy is in every way superior to native paddy, but that it is the growth of a higher system of cultivation than is generally prevalent in this country, which system is required to bring it to perfection and to prevent its deterioration. It is in the early stages of growth more delicate and requires more care, especially in sowing (so as to prevent its being sown too thickly) than is usually the case here. The seed is also liable to deterioration.

Further trials were made in India in 1871, 1872, 1873, and 1874. An account of them presents the same record of failures and of partial or complete success, but shows only a few new points of interest. Failures were due to destruction by heavy rains or by birds, rats, and insects, to the drought, to want of interest, and to causes unexplained, as in previous years.

Results go to show that the native rice will thrive under circumstances which would be highly predjudicial to Carolina rice, which must have a healthy soil resting on a moderately porous subsoil through which the irrigation water can pass. The roots of the Carolina plant are longer, showing that the plant feeds deep in the soil, while the short root of the native plant shows it to be a surface feeder.

It is evident, therefore, that land with a healthy surface only about 3 inches in depth can never produce a good crop of Carolina paddy, though it may produce fair crops of the country variety. In such soils the Carolina grows well enough until its roots begin to pass down into the unhealthy undersoil, when it sickens, turns yellow, and dies, while the country paddy, whose roots never reach this unhealthy undersurface, may thrive and yield fair results.

Deterioration of Carolina seed undoubtedly takes place when the crop is grown under very unfavorable circumstances, but this is likewise so with the seed of wheat and barley in India. Under suitable circumstances there is no reason why it should deteriorate. Much Carolina seed, however, becomes mixed with inferior native seed from carelessness on the part of the ryots. "Carolina rice is more subject to injury by salt water than native rice."

Although the Carolina method of cultivation was described in 1869 to Indian planters, very few of them seem to have followed it, most of them simply ignoring it and pursuing their own favorite methods, wholly foreign to its requirements. "Indian rice lives on the rainfall and Carolina rice upon irrigation." The crop should be tried along the canals, whereby a really valuable return might be made and money now sunk in canals might be saved.

Carolina rice grown in India is said to become changed in appearance and even to furnish several varieties of seed. It is recorded in the U. S. Department of Agriculture Report for 1877 that in the year 1871 several samples of seed were selected in Georgetown, S. C., for shipment to India, and that subsequently specimens of its Indian production were returned to the Department at Washington, whence they were sent to the planters who had furnished the seed, and who pronounced the seed so changed as to be hardly recognizable. This was in all probability due to the differences of soil, climate, and cultivation by which the plant had been affected in India. It may also have been due to careless cultivation or to accidental admixture with deteriorated "volunteer" rice, both from Carolina and native sowings, or to hybridization between Carolina and native rice when growing in adjacent fields, which might improve native varieties but would have a contrary effect upon Carolina seed. It is not recorded that any especial experiments in hybridization have ever been made in India.

Upon the whole, the attempted introduction of Carolina rice into

India can not be called a success. The seed seems to have been too widely and indiscriminately distributed. It might have been more satisfactory had but one or two well managed experiments been made in each district and a trustworthy record kept of the results. Past experiments, however, such as they are, have been recorded as data for future guidance, so that if this introduction is ever again undertaken previous mistakes may be avoided. There can, however, be no doubt that the experimental cultivation so widely carried on has diffused a supply of fresh seed over a large area of country, but whether or not the produce of this seed has been mixed up with and lost in the country varieties it is impossible to ascertain.

CEYLON.

This island does not produce rice for export, but imports largely from India. The average yield is comparatively small, being not more than 15 bushels to the acre, and crops are often lost by inundations or by carelessness. The methods of cultivation are variable and similar to native methods in India, very little manuring being done and instruments being of a primitive character. The upland rice of Ceylon is said to be more nutritious than any which is imported and the home product generally seems to be preferred in the island.

Interesting experiments in introducing Carolina rice into Ceylon were commenced in 1868, and are related by Mr. Liotard. The múdaliyar, or officer of Siyané Koraté, one of the provinces of the island, received from India a single pound of fresh Carolina seed and sowed it early in February, 1868. The drought was severe and he watered his field from a well. The plants grew well and were reaped in May, but produced only 2 pounds of paddy. These 2 pounds were sown October 2, 1868, and reaped in January, 1869, the yield being 3 pecks of paddy; fresh plants sprang out from the stalks left after the first reaping and produced a second crop which gave a quarter of a bushel more, making in all 1 bushel of paddy (weighing probably 45 pounds) from 2 pounds of seed. The whole bushel was carefully preserved and again sown November 6, 1869, and early in February, 1870, yielded 20 bushels. Out of these 20 bushels 1 bushel was sown June 1, 1870, in one field, and 8 bushels in another field in October, 1870, and the remaining 11 bushels were given to twenty-one cultivators for trial. From the first sown field 24 bushels were reaped in October, 1870, and the produce again distributed gratuitously to cultivators. From the second field, planted with 8 bushels October, 1870, 160 bushels were reaped early in February, 1871, all of which was distributed to various cultivators all over the island.

The Múdaliyar's own account of his experiment is as follows:

I have experienced that for the successful cultivation of this paddy it is necessary to have soft and continually moist ground. In fields near the banks of rivers or streams, or at the foot of hills, no artificial manuring is necessary, but they only require a good weeding when the plants are about a foot high. If this paddy is to be sown on a poor, sandy soil, it ought to be manured, either with bone dust, cow manure, ashes, or "keppetiya" leaves (which are to be had in abundance in almost all jungles) buried in the fields. But transplanting in either soil would yield crops of double the quantity expected. Out of my fields, without weeding or manuring, it gave me twentyfold and by weeding, bone dust, manuring, and transplanting, sixtyfold. This paddy ought to be sown very sparsely, so that the trees may not be closer than 6 inches from each other, as they shoot out a far larger number of young plants than the ordinary paddy, more particularly in the best soil; and if sown closer than described the paddy trees grow thin, fall off, and the whole crop gets spoilt. The excellence of this paddy will commence to manifest itself weekly after the sixth week, until they are reaped, which should not be endeavored to be done, as with the ordinary paddy, at once, as young plants of different growth are springing up from every paddy bush. They ought to be reaped as the paddy ripens from time to time. The stumps of these paddy trees are larger and stronger, the leaves broader, thicker, rough, and more dark green than ordinary paddy; the trees never fall down; they grow to the height of 4 and 5 feet; and when they commence to blossom they blossom at once; and when they commence to ripen they ripen at once, which is not the case with the paddy of this country; and they give different crops at different times, as the plants shoot out at different ages; and this paddy answers for all harvests in Siyané Koralé, namely the Maha, Sala, and Mutes harvests. According to the paddy cultivation in the Siyané Koralé, if this paddy is to be sown for the Maha harvest, they should be sown between October 1 and 5; if for the Sala harvest, on June 1 and 10; if for the Mutes harvest, on any early day in December, as the high water permits. If they are sown early for the Mutes harvest they can be reaped before the rising of the river. This paddy stands water and all other effects of the climate better than all the qualities of the native paddy. I found great difficulty in inducing the natives to try and cultivate this paddy, and they were very much disinclined to do so until they had seen the result of my cultivation, after which they flocked in for handfuls of seed paddy from me, and I think that two years hence there will be no other paddy cultivation in Siyané Koralé but that of Carolina paddy. This paddy is gradually improving in size after each cultivation of it, and they are the largest paddy now in existence in Ceylon, and it looks more like wheat than paddy, the husk being thinner and the paddy heavier than the paddy of this country, and when its rice is boiled for the table, it is much more white, gluey, and more heavy food than the Ceylon rice.

SIAM.

Until 1856 there existed a law in this country forbidding the exportation of rice until a three years' supply should be stored for home consumption, but in that year the law was repealed and a consequent impetus given to rice cultivation by the demand for Siamese rice from other countries, so that now Siam bids fair to be one of the largest rice producing and exporting countries of the world.

The demand for land for rice-growing, in which not only natives, but also thousands of Chinese are engaged, has caused the construction of canals for the double purpose of irrigation and communication through sections of the country which had lain uncultivated for centuries, thus opening to cultivation vast tracts of land previously idle. The surface of these plains is level, and the water in the canals rises and falls with the tide, and irrigation is easily performed. The soil is said to be so fertile that the rice " almost grows spontaneously." At present, however, not one-tenth of the available acreage of the country is under cultivation, mainly on account of want of communication with the capital, There is no scarcity of labor and when railroads shall have been built, a three or four fold increase in rice production may be looked for.

The rice fields are laid off into lots of about one-third of an acre each, surrounded by low banks of earth. There is a government tax of about 28 cents upon each field, but in order to encourage rice-growing the tax upon new fields is remitted for the first five years. Planting usually commences in June, when the first rains have sufficiently inundated the fields, and the system of transplanting is the one generally followed. There are three harvests a year, the rice planted in June, which is the best quality, known as " na-soon," and which forms the commercial crop, being harvested in September or October. The " midseason" rice is gathered in January, and the late or " heavy rice" in mid-January and February. A variety known as " na-moong" is sown broadcast upon the fields and allowed to grow without care, and in a few years yields an annual crop as wild rice, probably of inferior quality.

Implements are of a primitive sort. The rice is cut with sickles and thrashed by treading out with oxen, and for home consumption is cleaned up by the natives with mortar and pestle.

But if these primitive methods are used in a small way the commercial rice crop is very differently treated in Siam, for rice-cleaning is of extreme importance there and the milling and exportation of rice give a larger return of profit for capital invested in them than any other industry in the country. At Bangkok there were in October, 1890, twenty-three steam rice mills using the most modern machinery. The first steam rice mill in Siam was established by an American, who, not finding it profitable, abandoned the enterprise, but the business has since become exceedingly important, and new mills are constantly in construction. In 1888 eight new mills were erected by Chinese owners and two by English. The Chinese employ the best European engineers, and many of the mills are lighted by electricity and have double gangs of workmen, thus running day and night. The fuel used in these mills consists entirely of rice husks, consumed in furnaces especially built for the purpose. Five of the mills at Bangkok produce thoroughly cleaned rice, but most of the mills only perform a partial cleaning, leaving 20 per cent of paddy in the rice, which is thus said to keep better when shipped than if every grain were cleaned.*

FRENCH INDO-CHINA.

In Cochin China and Cambodia rice cultivation is the principal occupation of the people, demanding the least labor and giving the largest return. Both lowland and upland rice are grown, the former being the most common and, according to the soil upon which it is grown, it produces many varieties, so that over 200 have been enumerated. The method of transplanting is generally followed upon irrigated fields,

---

* Consular Reports, Nos. 95, July, 1888 (pp. 116 and 126, p. 384).

which are plowed by buffaloes, which can perform work in the thick mud of these fields that would be impossible for a horse or an ox.

In Cochin China over 9,000,000 piculs (1,200,000,000 pounds) are produced annually, and one-third of this crop suffices for the wants of the inhabitants, leaving the other two-thirds for exportation from Laïgon, the capital and principal port. The 800,000,000 pounds thus annually exported represent a value of 6,000,000 piasters, or $4,458,300.

The production in Cambodia is not stated. The farmers burn all grass, weeds, stubble, etc., and use the ashes as a fertilizer, and the rice crop is forced as much as possible, since the earliest crop brings the best price. The rice is said to be of excellent quality. Wild rice is also gathered, but only as a fodder for cattle, yet the poorer classes consume it and in years of drought, when the cultivated crop fails, the people generally are obliged to depend upon it.

In Annam, no rice is exported, as the crop fails to meet the home demand, but rice is imported from Laïgon or even from Hongkong.* Formerly almost all the rice consumed in Annam came from Tonkin, but high rates upon transportation by boats have driven the custom elsewhere.

In Tonkin the country is divided into the two natural divisions of the delta and the mountain region. The delta is almost entirely given up to rice-growing. Generally the harvest is sufficient for the home demand, and good harvests admit of the exportation of as much as 55,000,000 pounds a year, but in certain years the harvest is short and rice must be imported from Cochin China and Hongkong. The Annamites are said to excel in rice-growing. The delta lands generally yield two crops a year, the first in June and the second in November, and some fields are said to yield even three crops. Transplanting is done in March and in July. Most of the rice is of the lowland variety, though glutinous rice (*O. glutinosa*) is grown for distillation. The dikes between the rice fields form the common paths of the country. It is said that a good opportunity for French emigration is offered in Tonkin. Instruments and processes are primitive, and as yet there exist no rice-mills in French Indo-China.

THE STRAITS SETTLEMENTS.

The Malay Peninsula is covered with dense forests which it is difficult to clear for rice fields, so that these are generally situated near the older settlements. The Island of Singapore does not contain any soil suitable for rice.

---

* At the British port of Hongkong in China, there is no production of rice, but only trade in it. Ninety-five per cent of the rice handled there comes from Bangkok and Laïgon, the remainder coming from Hai Fong and Rangoon. Rice is shipped from Hongkong to the United States and Australia. All rice received at this port contains 20 per cent of paddy and is recleaned before reshipping. The laws of China forbidding the exportation of rice being still in force, the little Chinese rice that comes from Hongkong is practically smuggled out of the country. Most of it goes to Australia.

In June the rice nurseries are prepared upon moist land by careful hoeing and the seed sown broadcast at the rate of about three-fourths of a picul (100 pounds) to the acre. When the plants have grown about 7 or 8 inches in height water is let onto the beds to a depth of 3 or 4 inches. This depth is increased to 6 or 7 inches when the plants are a foot high, and the field is left in this condition until the time for transplanting, which is about the middle of August. The growing beds are from one-sixth to one-fourth of an acre in extent, and are carefully plowed and hoed. After the mid-August rains have set in the rice is transplanted, six or eight seedlings being set together in holes 4 inches deep and 1 foot apart, the roots of the seedlings being first dipped in a solution of powdered bone manure. If there is not too much rain, drought, or tempest the crop will generally turn out well, an average yield being about fiftyfold at the harvest in January or February. The process of cultivation is a slow one.

The rice is generally kept as paddy, being cleaned as wanted. The supply does not meet the demand and much rice has to be imported, but if the Malay natives had good plows and were taught the use of labor-saving machinery and had a little ambition, they could have no better occupation than rice cultivation. Territory which is now rice-importing could be made exporting or, at least, self-sustaining. First-class shipping facilities exist at Singapore. The rice grown at Wellesly is said to be of superior quality, and is generally supplied for the use of the passengers of the Peninsula and Oriental steamships, who prefer it to all other kinds.*

THE PHILIPPINE ISLANDS.

The home production is inadequate to supply the home demand, and so large quantities of rice are imported from Laïgon. The cultivation of rice in this enervating climate is primitive and laborious. The method followed resembles that followed throughout the East, yet presents one or two peculiarities. A square field of about an acre in extent is excavated in the soil to the depth of about a foot, and divided by walls of turf into smaller squares. The pathways upon these walls or dikes are often infested by a venomous serpent, known as the "paddy-snake," which attacks the cultivators, but does not harm the rice crop. After the rainy season has commenced, the earth in these squares is thoroughly plowed and the squares allowed to fill up with water. As soon as the mud has settled it is raked up again with rude wooden harrows. The seed is sown in a similar bed and allowed to grow until about 6 inches high, when the tops are cut off and the blade allowed to grow 2 inches more, after which they are transplanted at the end of July, the harvest being in December.†

---

* Consular Report No. 102, February, 1889 (p. 321).
† Consular Report No. 96, August, 1888 (p. 241).

Rice is cultivated in all parts of Persia wherever water is abundant, and thrives well near the rivers or perennial streams in the hot low-lands at the head of the Persian Gulf. It also thrives all over the Persian plateau at an elevation of from 1,000 to 8,000 feet, but best of all in the lowlands along the southern borders of the Caspian Sea. In some districts containing small streams only sufficient rice for home consumption is raised; other districts produce less than they consume; while others along the more important rivers produce rice in great abundance, and are able to supply the deficit in the rest of Persia, and even to have enough left for exportation. Unfortunately, the Caspian district is very unhealthy in summer, while the eastern part of the country, upon the borders of Afghanistan, though well watered, produces very little rice, and the Bam district, also well watered, is scantily populated, so that there is no cultivation and the water runs to waste. The usual Asiatic method of transplanting prevails in Persia, being performed from one to two months after the vernal equinox, *i. e.*, at the end of July or of August. The product is all lowland rice, raised by irrigation, as upland rice will not grow in Persia on account of insufficient rainfall. Implements and processes are of exceedingly primitive character. It is impossible to obtain correct figures of the annual production, as no agricultural statistics whatever exist, and even the population can only be estimated.*

ASIA MINOR.

In this country rice is grown to a limited extent in the province of Sivas, the crop, it is said, only amounting to about 35,000 pounds per year and being yellow and poor in quality. In Palestine no rice is grown at all. At Jerusalem Egyptian rice retails from 3 to 4 cents per pound and Italian at from 4 to 4½ cents, the duty upon imported rice being 8 per cent ad valorem and the export duty only 1 per cent. The consumption of rice in Turkey is enormous, but beyond the small quantity produced in Sivas and a still smaller quantity grown in eastern Roumelia, in European Turkey, none is produced in the country and the supply is imported from India, Egypt, and Italy, with a small proportion from England.

AFRICA AND THE INDIAN OCEAN.

Egypt.—Rice cultivation is extensively carried on upon the delta of the Nile, the best fields being in the neighborhood of Damietta, which, as well as Alexandria and Rosetta, is a commercial center for trade in rice. The production exceeds the home demand and the surplus mainly goes to Turkey. An account of the varieties of rice and of methods of cul-

* Consular Report No. 102, February, 1889.

tivation does not seem to have been published, though it is stated that American thrashers and rice-cleaning machines are used. The rich soil of the delta, with its annual alluvial deposits, is especially favorable to rice, which seems to be sown broadcast or otherwise while the land is still covered by the Nile's overflow. Rice is extensively cultivated by the native tribes upon both the east and west coasts of Africa, but the accounts given, mainly by travelers, are meager and unsatisfactory. In Sierra Leone there is found a peculiar variety known as "fundi," or "hungry rice," which is grown by certain native tribes. It has a semitransparent cardiform grain about as large as a mignonette seed. The ground is cleared for planting in May or June by burning down the copse wood and hoeing between the stumps, the seeds being then sown and lightly covered by the hoe. The plant grows to the height of about 18 inches and ripens in September, its very slender stems being bent to the ground by the weight of the grain. If allowed to become wet the grain adheres to its husk. It resembles a fine millet, and is probably a variety of upland rice.

Senegal.—The whole rice crop is generally consumed at home. In 1877 the value of the rice imported amounted to about $300,000, and of that exported to about $2,000.

French Soudan.—Rice is cultivated upon the upper and middle Niger. The natives do not embank their lands, but allow them to become overflowed, sowing broadcast in July and reaping in October. The quality of the Soudanese rice is said to be superior to that of India or of China, and the yield to be from 80 to 150 fold. As the country becomes more settled, the production will increase, prices will fall, and it is to be hoped methods of cultivation will improve.

Algeria and Tunis.—No rice is cultivated, though it would probably do well in both countries. It is said that in Algeria rice was grown before the French occupation of the country (1830), but was given up on account of the insalubrity of lowland cultivation. There seems to be, however, no reason why upland cultivation should not succeed in Algeria, and in Tunis as well, since both countries possess exceptional advantages as to climate and soil, and cereals generally do well there.

Madagascar.—Rice is grown in Madagascar, though not in sufficient quantity to satisfy the home demand, and therefore large quantities are imported into the island from southern Asia by foreign traders. The area under cultivation does not exceed a hundredth part of the total area of the island. In localities remote from centers of population cultivation is decreasing each year, principally, it is said, on account of the lack of good roads. Rice was formerly extensively cultivated and was at one time an important article of exportation, but the burning of the forests has so modified the climate that rice cultivation is now impossible in places where it once flourished. Implements and methods are primitive and there is great need of modern improvements, which may be soon expected, perhaps, since the island became a protectorate of France in 1885. The native method of cultivation is as follows: Each year a favorable spot of land is selected and the grass and bushes burned away; the land is then turned and the seed is sown during the rainy season and left to grow of itself. Next year a new spot is chosen and the process repeated, while the old field is abandoned. Near Jana-narivo, however, irrigable lands are prepared with great care and are planted after receiving a manuring from the pasturing of cattle and sheep.

Île de la Réunion.—This is a French colony, and rice and wheat, which formerly yielded 25 for 1, have been almost abandoned for the more lucrative cultivation of sugar cane. Rice is imported from India, and is said to be preferred by the inhabitants to the native article. Rice is also grown in Mauritius.

SOUTH AMERICA.

BRAZIL.

There is much land in this country well adapted to rice cultivation, especially in the valley of the Amazon, where, according to some authorities, rice is indigenous. Rice seems to grow wonderfully well in Brazil and to give a greater yield than in India. The rice of Maran-ham is said to rival that of South Carolina, and among the marshes of Matto Grosso or upon the banks of the San Francisco rice is said to yield fine crops without much labor or cultivation.

Very little cultivation, however, is carried on, and what there is is rudely and carelessly performed, no care being taken in the selection of seed or in the preparation of the soil. A portion of the crop is said to be cut green in harvesting, as there are not enough laborers to gather it quickly when ripe. Therefore rice is grown in small patches for home consumption only, most of it by Indians and small land-holders. Thrashing and cleaning are done as on a small scale in the United States. No rice is exported, but large quantities are imported from Europe.

UNITED STATES OF COLOMBIA.

In this country as much rice is consumed per capita as in India or China, yet the production falls far short of the requirements of the people. A certain variety of rice is grown, having a grain so small that no machinery can be found to clean it, so cleaning must be done by hand in the old-fashioned way. There would be a good opportunity for the sale of proper American machinery in Colombia. Cultivation is intelligently carried on, and two crops a year are gathered in some places. Much rice is imported from Rangoon. The South Carolina rice is too high in price for this market.*

* Consular Report No. 62, March, 1886.

In Peru rice cultivation is carried on in a very primitive manner, and better results might be obtained if the present water supply were utilized with judgment. It is said that the water which now runs to waste might, with better methods, suffice to double the present production.

AUSTRALASIA AND THE PACIFIC.

AUSTRALIA.

In New South Wales rice is not grown in sufficient quantity to form an article of commerce. Several varieties have been successfully grown in the northern part of the colony, from 30° to 32° south latitude, upon land subject to overflow, but in general the high cost of labor and the limited area are obstacles to profitable cultivation.

The following view of the subject of rice cultivation in this colony is condensed from a letter from Messrs. Robert Harper & Co., of Sydney, June 24, 1891, to the editor of the "Agricultural Gazette," of New South Wales, and published in that journal for August, 1891, vol. II. part 12, page 482:

We are pleased to give any information we can upon a matter of such importance to the coastal districts as new crop. At the same time we would suggest the wisdom of caution, both in forming opinions and in action, for while we trust that rice-growing will be a success in our colony, there are certain considerations which seem to throw a doubt upon it. The most important of these considerations is that in those countries where rice is now grown they possess a climate admirably suited to its production, soil equally suited, and an experience of centuries in growing, and yet at the prices obtained it yields but a fair living to native races, which work for a mere pittance. It is true that against this there are the freight and duty, but the freight from many ports of the East is now no more than from the River Clarence to Sydney, and we fear that even the £3 per ton duty will not cover the difference in the cost of labor; but if this duty should provide a profit for the grower here, it has then to be remembered that at any moment it may be removed, in which case we feel sure the East will win in the competition.

However, we quite agree that the crop is worthy of a trial, and the foregoing remarks are only meant to induce caution, and thus prevent the loss which will ensue from rashness.

It is rather a mistake to cultivate Patna rice, since about 100 tons would cover the consumption of that quality in this colony for twelve months. At one time Patna was a rice largely consumed, it being the favorite of both Chinese and Europeans; but for a number of years the Chinese in Australia have been supplied by grain grown in their own country and are becoming more and more bound to it. The Europeans, on the other hand, left Patna in favor of Java rice—a round grain—years ago, but for a number of years past have gone from the Java to a similar grain grown in Japan, which yields a good boiling rice, and at the same time, under the elaborate machinery now used in good rice mills, turns out a very pretty, highly polished sample. Practically, then, only two sorts of rice have been largely used in this colony for years, namely, "Japan" and "China," and it is to the Japan that we would recommend growers in New South Wales to give their attention. The reason we select it in preference to the China rice is that there is a considerably larger consumption, and because Chinese houses in Sydney, which are in some cases simply branches of Chinese houses in China, would not try locally-grown rice, even were it somewhat cheaper than imported, but would, under the instructions of their head firms in China, continue to import from them, at any rate for some years. It seems, then, that rice may be exported from China to Chinese consumers in other countries. Then, again, the Japanese grain should suit the climate, as many parts of Japan fairly represent the climate of the north coast districts of New South Wales, and Japanese rice grown in these districts would find a ready market at Sydney, provided it were of good quality and the price offered to compete with imported rice would pay the grower.

This price for rice in the husk would depend, first, on the cost of husking; second, upon loss in weight, and third, upon the current value of similar rice imported, which varies from year to year. An actual test with the grain itself, in husking and polishing, would be necessary before the price could be fixed. There are rice mills in Sydney where the grain might be dressed for growers or bought in the husk. The general price for dressing is from £1 to £2 per ton, but that is for rice from which the outer husk has already been removed in the East.

At this time the selling price of China rice at Sydney was from £18 to £18 10s., and for Japan rice from £16 10s. to £17 10s. per ton, duty paid. The market for Japan rice was a declining one and the price of China rice was higher than usual, it being often cheaper than Japan rice.

Mr. W. Newton, of Coopernook House, Manning River, New South Wales, has made a successful experiment in growing Patna rice in this colony, harvesting fully 60 bushels to the acre, and he explains his method of cultivating it in the "Gazette" for December, 1891, page 727, as follows:

The Patna rice will grow either in or out of water, but must be attentively cultivated and weeds kept down. In experimenting with small quantities the seed should be sown in drills and given the same cultivation as sorghum. Lines should be 18 inches apart and the drills should receive three or four seeds each and should be 7 inches apart, the seed being covered 3 or 4 inches deep with a light harrow-hoe. Before planting, the seed should be soaked in water for sixteen or eighteen hours and then planted at once and the rice will be above ground in two weeks. The proper time for planting is in August or September (i. e., in late winter or early spring in the southern hemisphere, where our seasons are reversed), so that by early planting the rice may get a good start before the summer weeds begin to grow.

Mr. Newton is of the opinion that by early planting two crops might be harvested in New South Wales as well as in Queensland, where the same seed is used. When the rice is ripe and fit for harvesting, the straw is quite green and soft, so that if sown early the rice roots will shoot out a second crop. Rice may be planted any time before Christmas (i. e., midsummer) and one first-class crop obtained. The rice, when cut, should be harvested just as wheat or oats before being stacked, in order to prevent heating, since the straw is green. An ordinary wheat-thrashing machine may be used and the straw used as fodder for horses and cattle. Rice may also be sown broadcast, a harrow being run over the field once a week for the first month after sowing in order to kill weeds. This destroys all native grass without injuring the rice, as when once shot, it roots rapidly and is not easily torn up. The first crop matures in about five months.

Queensland has a soil better suited to the cultivation of rice than

New South Wales, as it lies farther to the north and is more tropical. There are in the colony immense tracts of swamp land now lying unimproved where lowland rice might be successfully grown. At present, however, the production is but small and mostly in the hands of the Chinese. Since 1886 there has been a falling off in the cultivation, owing to carelessness, it is said, in the selection of seed. The average yield per acre, however, is good, being over 32 bushels in 1890, and thus testifying to the suitability of the soil. With care and good methods there is no reason why a return of from 60 to 70 bushels might not be expected. Rice is now imported from Hongkong, but with increased cheap production the importation might be stopped. The seed used in Queensland is of Chinese origin and seems to have deteriorated, so that a change is desirable and the use of the Indian or the Siamese seed has been advised. Patna rice should do well in the colony. The use of American rice-cleaning machinery is also advocated.

The other Australian colonies apparently produce no rice.

In New Caledonia, a French colony, the soil and climate are well adapted to rice, but up to 1888 not more than 200 tons annually had ever been produced. The streams of the colony are not well adapted for irrigation, and thus cultivation is not remunerative, in addition to which the crops are devastated by locusts. The rice produced, however, is of superior quality. The "caugh," or red mountain rice, grows on the slopes of the interior, but is almost uncultivated and is of inferior quality. The annual consumption is about 800 tons, three quarters of which is imported from Hongkong via Sidney.*

THE SANDWICH ISLANDS.

Rice cultivation flourishes in these islands and is second in importance only to that of sugar cane. The climate of Hawaii is particularly favorable to rice of superior quality, and the evenness of temperature permits the raising of two crops a year without strain on the soil. The rice fields are confined to the lowlands where abundant irrigation may be obtained, or to slight elevations where artesian wells may be operated. These are the highest-priced lands in the Kingdom and, owing to water facilities and nearness to the market, command from $100 to $200 per acre. They are generally leased on 5 to 20 years' contract, in lots of an acre each, at from $15 to $30 per acre. The total area of rice lands in the Kingdom is about 4,700 acres, and the cultivation is almost entirely in the hands of Chinese farmers.

The fields are prepared by thorough working and soaking, and the seed is sown broadcast. When 6 inches high the rice is transplanted in rows about 6 inches apart and is then kept continuously flooded with water, not more than 6 inches deep, for about 5 months, when the grain forms and begins to harden. The water is then drawn off and the grain allowed to ripen. It is then cut with the sickle and thrashed by tread-

---

*Consular Report No. 102.

ing out with horses, winnowed, and sent to the mills at Honolulu, where American machinery is in operation. All plows and other implements are of American make. Some very handsome samples of rice from the Sandwich Islands were displayed at the Paris Exposition of 1889.*

EUROPE.

FRANCE.

This is not a rice-growing country, though the cultivation of rice has been experimented with at various times in the department of the Gironde, upon the coast of the Bay of Biscay, and in the department of the Aude and the Gard, upon the Mediterranean coast, but without success. The only application of rice cultivation in France seems to be the utilization of the salt marshes of the Camergne. Rice is imported into France from South Carolina, Italy, Japan, and India, and is cleaned in mills at Paris, Bordeaux, Havre, and Nantes. It is admitted duty free if intended for the manufacture of starch. Several of the French colonies, however, produce good rice, the most important of these having been described above.

ITALY.

Rice-growing is of ancient date in this country and has now become a profitable industry. Its area, once limited by legislation, has greatly increased since the restriction was removed several years ago, so that the total crop is now more than sufficient to meet the home demand, and a surplus is left for exportation. Piedmont and Lombardy are the principal rice-growing provinces, and there is also some cultivated in the marshes of Sicily, around Catania.

In general, cultivation is carefully conducted and has received much attention from scientist, while it benefits by the superior system of irrigation existing in the country.

The rice fields of northern Italy may be divided into two classes, permanent and temporary. The permanent fields, "*risage da zappa,*" are restricted to low, marshy localities, unsuited to the growing of any other crops, and which, in many cases, have regularly been cultivated in rice for a long series of years. Some of these fields, on account, perhaps, of specially favorable conditions of soil, or because they have been renewed by alluvial deposits or by periodical manuring, have remained in good condition for a long time; but others, under less favorable circumstances or from want of care in cultivation, have become much less productive than they formerly were. Some of these latter fields are still cultivated in rice, notwithstanding their failing condition, either for reasons of economy or because the Italian farmers, who are reluctant to adopt new methods, find it more convenient to retain the old system.

---

* Consular Report No. 69, October, 1886.

The temporary fields, "*risage da vicenda*," are found among the better soils of irrigated districts and are subjected to systems of rotation. a practice as old as the introduction of rice into the country. These systems are many and various; in one, maize, with barn-yard manure or guano, alternates with the rice; in another, clover, well fertilized, or wheat and clover planted together are followed by pasture. rice being planted the third year. A nine years' rotation is also mentioned, generally taking the following order: First year. wheat. with grass seed: 2d. 3d, and 4th, hay; 5th, 6th. and 7th. rice: 8th and 9th, maize. this last being sometimes replaced by other crops.

The rice grown in Italy is almost all lowland rice. It is said that a Chinese variety of seed is preferred, since it ripens in from one hundred to one hundred and twenty days after sowing, and fifteen or twenty days sooner than the Japanese seed, and is therefore less liable to attack by " brusone."

In Italy a clay soil, having a small proportion of sand at the surface and some humus. is considered the best for rice. It is also stated that an abundance of nitrogen and of potassium salts, with some phosphoric acid. is desirable. but that too great a proportion of lime is injurious. Clay soils, being but slightly penetrable by water. require less irrigation. Rice does not bear subterraneous infiltration. as the water thus supplied to the plant is too cold and impedes its growth.

The system of cultivation followed in Italy resembles that followed in South Carolina rather than that of Asiatic countries, and transplanting is apparently never performed. The land is carefully leveled. slopes or hillsides being terraced, after the Chinese fashion, and the embankments are generally about 2 feet high. Connections are established between compartments or fields at different levels so that the water may flow from the higher to the lower level. Italian rice fields are always so arranged that the water may be constantly flowing through them with a gentle motion. not strong enough to disturb the tender young plants, yet enough to keep the supply always fresh and prevent stagnation, a fruitful source of malaria in the Italian climate. All trees are removed from the immediate vicinity of the rice fields. since their shade is considered hurtful to the crop. The fields are generally left dry during the winter, though in some cases very muddy water is left upon them for the purpose of improving them by alluvial deposit or raising their level. Plowing is generally done in March or April or. sometimes. in the autumn. In marshy localities, too wet for plowing, the land is broken up by the spade. a tedious and unhealthy process. The plowing is never very deep. After the ground has been broken up the fields are flooded, partly in the regular process of preparation and partly, also, to verify the levels and to consolidate the banks by pressure of the water.

Fertilizers are also applied to the soil. When rotation has been practiced, especially when meadow or pasture-land has entered therein, the soil is considered to be sufficiently fertile, so that additional manures might be prejudicial rather than of benefit. In such cases manuring is sufficient once in two years. If cereals—for instance, wheat or maize—which exhaust the soil have been grown, manuring must be done every year, and it is a practice in Italy to alternate the manures as well as the crops. Superphosphate of lime and calcined bone are often used and are much appreciated, as are also guano and guano phosphates. Another fertilizer in common use is the ashes of various plants. Young wheat, oats or rye, red clover, turnips, or chick-peas are also grown and plowed under as green fertilizers.

The rice fields having been prepared, and the soil brought to a state of thick, soft mud, the sowing commences, generally about the last of March or the first of June. New fields are sown earliest and those one year or more old later, as the soil is benefited by a more or less prolonged exposure to the heat of the sun. From 3 to 4 bushels of seed per acre are used, according to the state of the soil, sowing being done broadcast or in furrows and the seed being prepared by soaking in water for twenty-four hours. The sprouts appear above the surface in from twelve to twenty days after sowing, being later in appearance when the seed is older or the water colder. Should no sprouts appear before the twenty-fifth day, the field is resowed. At the time of sowing the field is covered with a layer of water, and when the sprouts appear the water is drawn off until it is only about a centimeter (0.39 inch) deep, thus allowing the warm earth to more easily develop the plant. It is easy to maintain this level against loss by evaporation by the system of constant but gentle flow above mentioned. The water should not be many degrees colder than the atmosphere, and in many cases percolating filters are used. As the plants increase in height the depth of the water is increased with them, so that merely their tops show above it, the water being always let in very gently. When a depth of from 15 to 30 centimeters (say 6 to 12 inches) is reached, the level is kept constant, the lower level being used upon cold and the higher upon warmer soils. The fields are kept flooded until the plants flower, which is from the middle of July to the middle of August. Weeding commences in June, and is done by men or women who wade in the water, using the hoe or pulling up the grass by hand. There are generally two weedings, about three weeks apart. When flowering occurs, the low level of the water is replaced by regular but abundant irrigation at intervals of a few days. When the head forms and begins to ripen the land is drained, and in from ten to fifteen days the crop is ready for the harvest. This occurs in northern Italy generally during the latter half of September, and the crop is cut with the scythe or reaping hook. The plant is cut a constant length of 18 inches and the stubble is afterwards turned under by the plow as a fertilizer.

Thrashing is generally done in a primitive manner by treading by oxen or horses, though in some cases thrashing machines are used, and the grain is subsequently dried by exposure to the sun. The method of curing practiced in the United States does not seem to be followed. Husking is often done at small mills attached to the farm, or the crop is sold as paddy for exportation.

A system of insurance of the rice crop against damage by frost is practiced in Italy, the premium being from 6 to 9 per cent of the gross value of the crop.

DISEASES OF RICE.

These have been especially studied by Prof. Santo Garovaglio, of Pavia, whose researches have been published.* The conclusions of these researches show that many of the diseases to which rice is subject in Italy are due to the microscopic fungi belonging to the group of *Spheriaciæ*, and more particularly to the genus *Pleospora*, which is analogous to that producing certain diseases of the vine, the mildew and rust of wheat and maize, the potato disease. etc.

This parasite is found in the deepest recesses of the plant and under favorable conditions feeds upon its juices, impeding its growth and the formation of the head. The brusone is the most serious form of this disease and often destroys a crop in a few days. It first appears by showing a deep green color in the cavities of the leaves and stems, which gradually spreads over the whole plant. The spots become yellow and then brown and collect at the nodes of the stems and the joints of the leaves just above the water, and then afterwards below its level. Later the plant withers and dies and nothing is left but the stalk, which has a scorched appearance, whence the name brusone.

The circumstances which favor the development of the disease are said to be the irregularity of summer weather, especially sudden changes of temperature in July and August, which produce a general attack of brusone all over the country. Other causes are the presence of an excess of organic matter in the soil. dense shade by trees near the rice fields, or the use of very cold or impure water in irrigating. Brusone is said to be comparatively rare upon strong clay soils and more frequent upon loose soils containing too much sand. Remedies have not been suggested.†

SPAIN.

Rice is said to have been introduced into Spain by the Moors at a very early day. Its cultivation, however, appears to have died out and to have been reintroduced in recent times.

The most important rice-growing district of the country is in the

---

* Triennial Archives of the Laboratory of Cryptogamic Botany at Pavia, 1871–1871.

† This account of Italian rice-growing has been condensed from a Monograph upon the Cultivation of Rice in Italy and from Tropical Agriculture, by P. L. Simmonds, London. 1877.

province of Catalonia, upon the delta of the Ebro, between the mountains and the Mediterranean, and some cultivation is also carried on in Valencia, farther southward. The following account of cultivation upon the Ebro delta is mainly taken from a report by the French vice-consul at Tortosa, M. Ducloux, published in the Bulletin of the French Ministry of Agriculture for 1889.

The area of the delta is about 30,000 hectares (74,130 acres or 116 square miles), and is divided into almost equal parts by the Ebro. The southern part, upon the right bank of the river, is irrigated by a canal which is derived from the river above Tortosa. Rice has been cultivated here since 1860, the first rice fields having been established, it is said, by Frenchmen. The cultivation was so successful that the Spaniards took it up and so extended it that land soon rose in price from 16 to 60 francs per hectare ($1.25 to $4.70 per acre) up to 800 and 1,000 francs per hectare ($62.50 to $78 per hectare). The part of the delta north of the river is still without irrigation and remains a sandy desert covered with saline efflorescence, while upon the right bank there are fertile rice fields. The whole surface of the delta forms a vast plain, which at no point rises more than 4 meters (13 feet) above sea level, and which here and there has depressions formerly filled with salt water and now containing layers of crystallized salt utilized by the peasants. There are also pools communicating with the sea, in which there is a thick vegetation of marine plants, and which are well stocked with fish, while there are also marshes and peat beds.

The soils of the rice fields may be divided into three classes—the rich loamy soils, the medium, and the sandy soils. The first are composed of fine alluvium deposited by the river, and contain neither pebbles, gravel, nor coarse sand. They are poor in organic matter, and consist of at least one-half pure clay, and are difficult to render productive. In the rainy season the water penetrates this soil but imperfectly, remaining at the surface and forming a sticky mud, which becomes very hard upon drying, so that the plow is often powerless to break it up, although by contraction in drying it becomes full of fissures. Upon this soil, which contains elements of fertility in abundance, all sorts of crops have been tried, and rice alone has given satisfactory results. In the first years of trial yields of 60 and 70 hectoliters per hectare (from 69 to 80 bushels per acre) were obtained without the use of fertilizers, but of course this yield could not be kept up without returning to the soil the elements taken from it by the crop.

The medium soils are better provided with organic detritus, and present an advantageous mixture of clay, sand, and lime, so that many plants may be successfully grown upon them, yet rice does not seem to succeed in these soils, probably on account of the slight elevation of their surface above the underlying water layer.

The sandy soils, almost as poor in humus as the clay soils, are yet composed of a mixture well enough adapted for cultivation, and all sorts of crops grow well on them.

The mean annual temperature of the region of the Delta is 17.6° C. (63.7° F.), the highest observed temperature being 41° (105.8° F.), and the lowest 2° C. (+28.4° F.). The year averages 247 cloudless days, 44 cloudy days, and 74 days of rain. The annual rainfall is 427 millimeters (16.81 inches) and the mean daily evaporation is 8.8 millimeters (0.35 inch), the annual hydroscopic mean being 64. The south wind is the prevailing wind, and blows through the hot season. From December to March, inclusive, the north wind generally prevails with violence.

The area of irrigable territory at Tortosa, Amposta, and San Carlos de la Rapita, upon which, after investigation, the Government has authorized rice cultivation, is about 12,000 hectares (29,652 acres, or about 46.3 square miles), yet through various causes the area annually occupied does not exceed 5,000 hectares (12,355 acres, or 19.3 square miles). It is difficult to fix the actual value of land upon the Delta with any accuracy, as there are no buyers, yet 250 francs per hectare ($19.52 per acre) is probably not far from the actual value. Rents have notably diminished in the last fifteen years, but not in proportion to the value of real estate. In 1889 they averaged 70 francs per hectare ($5.47 per acre) per annum. At San Carlos the rice fields were exempt from taxes at this time.

There are other rice lands outside of the Ebro district, in territory declared to be agricultural colonies, where the cultivators are exempt from real estate and other taxes, and even from military service.

The fee payable to the Royal Ebro Canal Company is fixed at a uniform rate of one-ninth of the value of the rice crop standing in the fields at the moment of harvest. This system is an evident obstacle to intensive cultivation, and its replacement by some other system is desirable. Certain owners have arranged with the company to pay a fee of 54 francs per hectare ($4.22 per acre) instead of the above proportion. The waters of the principal canal are distributed to the various rice fields through the instrumentality of a syndicate, which regulates their use and maintains secondary canals, roads, and canals for drainage. The expenses of this syndicate are paid by proprietors of rice fields at a pro rata, according to the surface cultivated by each, the expense amounting to about 16 francs per hectare ($1.25 per acre) annually.

Cultivation commences in the autumn as soon as the preceding harvest has been gathered and removed. The first operation is to burn the stubble and straw remaining upon the ground, after which the soil is plowed deeply. This work, together with the repairing of embankments and ditches, occupies until January, or sometimes until February. Before the flooding of the fields, which is in April, the soil receives a second or even a third working, after which the surface is made as level as possible, sometimes the level of the water being used as a guide, as in Italy. The seed is then sown broadcast, the soil having been stirred up under water, about 160 liters of seed being used to the hectare (1.84 bushels to an acre). During germination and the first few days of vegetation the water is only 2 or 3 centimeters (about an inch) in depth, but this depth is increased as the plant develops until it amounts to 20 centimeters (nearly 8 inches). As the rice grows the weeds invade the beds, so that weeding must be frequently done from the 1st of June to the end of August. The commonest grasses infesting the rice beds are barnyard grass (*Panicum crus-galli*) and a Spanish grass called "goose-tongue" (*Potamogeton fluitans*), which entangles the stalks of the rice. When this latter grass is very thick the only remedy is to let the field lie fallow for a year, with frequent workings.

The crop ripens about the middle of September. In fields still covered by water the stalks are cut by the sickle and carried away for thrashing, but in dry fields they are dried in the sun upon the stubble. Thrashing is done by treading out by oxen, mules, or horses upon floors of beaten clay, and the grain spread in the sun to dry, after which it is taken to the mills at Tortosa and Vinaroz. Spanish paddy weighs about 50 to 55 kilograms to the hectoliter (about 39 to 43 pounds per bushel) and yields, under the cleaning process used, 63 per cent of white rice.

The above-mentioned yield of 60 to 70 hectoliters per hectare above mentioned as being obtained in the first years of cultivation can not be kept up without renovation of the soil by fertilizers. After the first three or four seasons it begins to lessen each year, even upon the best cared for fields, and finally drops to 28 and 30 hectoliters (32 to 34½ bushels per acre). When this occurs fertilizers must be used, or the field must be allowed to lie fallow or must be improved by "colmatage," *i. e.*, the deposit of alluvial matter from the river, or a greater yield than 30 hectoliters can not afterward be counted upon.

If the maximum yield of 70 hectoliters should be maintained, valued at 14 francs per hectoliter, or 980 francs per hectare ($76.54 per acre), there will be a net profit of 494 francs per hectare ($42.63 per acre), which is considered a good return. With a yield of 35 hectoliters, or half as much as the above, the profit is almost nothing, and without fertilizers a yield of 28 or 30 hectoliters results in actual loss. This is the principal cause of the crisis in the Delta. Certain well-to-do proprietors understand this and maintain superior fields by the use of Peruvian guano, but unfortunately the majority of the farmers lack capital with which to buy fertilizers.

In Valencia, says Mr. Mertens, in Consular Report No. 105, May, 1889, rice is sown in March, and the seedlings are transplanted in the Asiatic manner, when from 20 to 30 centimeters high (8 to 12 inches), which is in May or June, and the crop is gathered in August or September, the rice then having an average height of 1 meter (39.37 inches). About 25 per cent of the crop is shipped to Cuba, the rest being consumed in the country itself. In bad harvest years foreign rice is imported, although foreign rice always finds a market at Valencia when prices range lower than that of the home production. There are about 120 rice mills in the province. most of them being worked by water power.

Many other countries produce rice in small quantities for home consumption, but the foregoing are the chief producers or those of most interest. It is unfortunate that many countries, such as Portugal, for example, where the mode of cultivating rice might prove instructive, do not publish any account of their proceedings.

TABLE IV.—*Production of rice in the United States.*

States.	1850.	1860.	1870.	1880.	
	Pounds.	Pounds.	Pounds.	Acres.	Pounds.
Alabama	2,312.252	493.465	222.945	1.579	810,889
Arkansas	63.179	16.831	73.021		
California		2.140			
Florida	1,075.090	223.704	401.687	2.551	1.294.677
Georgia	38,950.691	52.507.652	22.277.380	34.973	25.369.687
Kentucky	5.088				
Louisiana	4,425.349	6.331.257	15.854.012	42.000	23,182.311
Michigan		716			
Minnesota		3.286			
Mississippi	2,719.856	809.082	374.627	3.501	1,718,951
Missouri	700	9.767			
North Carolina	5.465.868	7.593.976	2.059.281	10.846	5.609,191
South Carolina	159.930.613	119,100.528	32.304.825	78.388	52,077.515
Tennessee	258.854	40.372	3.399		
Texas	88,203	26.031	63.844	335	62,152
Virginia	17.154	8.225			
United States	215.313.497	187,167,032	73.635.021	174.173	110,131,373

Production of rice in the United States in 1889.

States.	Acres.	Crop in pounds.	Value.
Alabama	810	399.270	$13.797
Arkansas	9	7,110	367
Florida	1.787	1.011,805	36,174
Georgia	18.126	14,057.872	446.919
Louisiana	84.472	76,221.636	2.204.792
Mississippi	1.543	676.746	24.964
North Carolina	12.241	5.846.404	162,491
South Carolina	43,237	31,689.497	1,057,157
Texas	178	108,423	4,452
Virginia	3	360	6
United States	162,406	130.019,123	3.951,119

RICE SOILS OF SOUTH CAROLINA.

By Milton Whitney, M. S.

IDLE LAND.

There are at present in South Carolina, and doubtless the same conditions hold in other rice-growing States, thousands of acres of the finest rice lands which have been abandoned and are now lying idle. The conditions which have led to this are interesting to a student of social science, and while they are discouraging to many of the present owners of the land they undoubtedly offer certain advantages to intelligent and well-to-do planters who have sufficient capital to invest in rice culture.

The cultivation of rice is a very expensive undertaking, and, as a rule, it can be carried on much more economically on a large scale than on a small scale, and probably for the production of no other purely agricultural crop are capital and strict business methods so necessary as for the production of rice by the method of water-culture.

The principal cause which has brought about the existing conditions of things and has caused the abandonment of so much rice land, is the lack of capital, due to the heavy losses sustained by the planters during the late war. Not only did the war leave the planters without working capital and without means to employ labor, but during their absence the freshets had broken the dikes and filled up the canals and ditches so that it would have required a considerable outlay of money to have put the rice plantations in their former condition. When the cotton-planter returned to the plantation after the war he could begin on a much smaller scale, with perhaps only a few acres under cultivation and one or two mules to work the crop, gradually increasing and extending his operations as the profits on his crops came in. The rice planter could not begin in this small way, for the dikes must all be repaired and the canals and ditches put in order before it would be safe or practicable to cultivate any single field on the plantation.

The rice lands had to be mortgaged, and these mortgages increased from time to time to secure the most pressing needs of support, and these mortgages are still held in the Charleston banks, no one caring to foreclose and get property which is practically unimproved and for which there is no sale, as there is very little local capital in the State to invest in the improvements which would be necessary to restore the land to a

77

condition fit and safe for cultivation. Lands, which were formerly worth $200 or $300 per acre, are now worth no more than $20 or $30, and where the dikes have been washed away and the canals and ditches filled up and the lands abandoned they can often be purchased for $1 per acre. Planters who purchased only a few years ago, while land values were still high and crop prices good, giving mortgages for part of the purchase money, have been unable, owing to the subsequent and unlooked for decline in land value and in market value of the crop, resulting from the wonderful advances in industrial lines and the cheapening of the freight rates from all over the world, to pay the interest on the debt and maintain the plantation in good condition. More money has been raised to meet current expenses, and finally the heavy mortgage has been such a burden that it could not be longer borne and the lands are abandoned and thrown on to the market. There is, therefore, no lack of the best rice lands in the State with good water facilities, which can be purchased for a merely nominal sum.

INEFFICIENT LABOR.

Another fact which has brought about the present condition of affairs and explains in part why so much of the rice land is abandoned, is the scarcity and inefficiency of the negro labor, by which practically all of the field work has been done. The phosphate industry along the coast in South Carolina and in Florida has drawn large numbers of these negroes away from the rice fields, attracting them by higher wages and what they consider a more independent life. It is difficult to secure enough labor to handle the crops, and the negroes who remain on the plantations are not as steady, as efficient, or as reliable as the older generations were before the war. With the phosphate works almost in sight of their dwellings, and an abundance of fish and game, and a mild climate, making it easy to live, they are so irresponsible that it is difficult to control the labor. They are very unwilling to work in the ditches and canals, and it is almost impossible to keep the ditches and canals clean and of a proper depth by the available negro labor. Formerly such work was done in the fall and winter seasons, and the dikes, ditches, and canals were repaired and put in order for the next year's crop. It is difficult and expensive to control the labor to do this work now, and the canals are not as wide nor as deep as formerly, and the drains can not be kept open for the proper distribution of water.

It is very expensive to keep up the dikes so as to secure the crops from freshets. Formerly the State helped build and maintain these dikes, upon the height and stability of which along the river fronts these rice lands very largely depend, but now it is left to the individual planters and there is more disaster from freshets. There is opportunity here for the introduction of improved machinery which would do away with much of this inefficient labor. Small steam dredging machines or steam shovels could be used to build up and repair the dikes, to widen and deepen the canals, and even to clean out the larger drains. The machinery could be mounted on large flats, similar to those used for transporting the crop from the field, and two or three men with such dredges could do the work of a large number of laborers, and do it better and more quickly, under the conditions which prevail, than it could be done with shovels. These dredges could be owned by the larger planters, or they could be owned by an individual or a stock company who would contract with the planters to do a certain piece of work or to maintain the dikes, canals, and ditches in a certain specified condition.

Machinery could also be used in the preparation of the land and in the cultivation and harvesting of the crop. It must be understood that these rice lands are perfectly level, and are divided usually into rectangular fields of about 20 acres, with low dikes or embankments around each, sufficiently broad on top for a horse, and often for a cart or wagon, to travel on. There is no reason why steam machinery should not be used on these fields under the peculiar conditions of rice culture, especially as, unlike many other staple crops, rice culture is more economical on a large scale than on a small scale. It is not at all unusual to find plantations of 10,000 acres, with perhaps half of this amount of land available for rice culture, in a narrow strip along the river front from half a mile to a mile wide.

It is therefore quite possible for anyone starting in with sufficient capital to secure the finest rice lands at a very low price and by the introduction of improved methods, and especially by the introduction of improved machinery, to be largely independent of the scarcity and inefficiency of the labor.

LOW PRICE OF RICE.

Another condition which has tended to discourage the present owners of these abandoned lands is the low price of rice, due to the competition from abroad, made possible by the splendid facilities for transportation in the introduction of steam. This has acted in all branches of agriculture. Wheat brought a good market price while all required for home consumption had to be raised within hauling distance by teams, but this marvelous improvement in the means for transportation, which makes it cheaper to bring a barrel of flour from the far West to New York than to haul it up from the cars to your dwelling after it arrives, has opened up vast areas in the West for the production of wheat, and the home producer is no longer protected by the cost of transportation from a distance, and the price of wheat has fallen as low as 65 and 70 cents per bushel. The same causes have operated to lower the price of rice by bringing into competition the far off Eastern countries. There has been a revolution in industrial lines which has, from time to time, demoralized agriculture, and with her slow methods it is taking a long time to recover from this and to adjust herself to the wonderful advancement in industrial pursuits.

CLIMATIC CONDITIONS—METHODS OF CULTIVATION.

The climatic conditions prevailing along the coast in our southern States, and particularly in South Carolina, are eminently adapted to rice culture, and the admirable methods followed in the improvement of the plants by the selection of seed have given the South Carolina rice a world-wide reputation, which it justly deserves. By the introduction of machinery the production of rice can be cheapened and made more secure, and it only awaits the introduction of capital and of strict business enterprise and methods to revive the industry and to extend it far beyond what it ever has been.

The soils of the rice lands are very rich alluvial deposits, brought down from the up-country and deposited along the low level terraces at high tide or when the water overflows its banks during the time of freshets. There is a fall line running nearly parallel with the coast along the Atlantic seaboard, which in South Carolina is about 130 or 150 miles inland from the coast. On one side of this line are the hard crystalline rocks of the Piedmont plateau, and on the lower side the soft, unconsolidated material of more recent geological formations from the Cretaceous to the present time. A number of important cities are located along this fall line, such as Baltimore, Washington, Richmond, Raleigh, Columbia, and Augusta, the locations offering the advantages of water power on one side of the city for manufacturing purposes, and of navigation on the other side, with direct water communication with the sea, for the products of the manufacturers. Along this line the water falls over the crystalline rocks into the soft and unconsolidated material of the more recent geological formations, through which it has worn its way into a nearly level bed for 150 or 200 miles to the ocean. There is a regular ebb and flow of the tide sufficient for irrigating purposes over a large part of this distance, although there is such a volume of water coming down that, except on rare occasions, when the river is very low, or of continued strong east wind, the salt water does not extend inland more than a very few miles from the mouth of the rivers.

The water comes down laden with the most fertile portion of the soils of the up-country. The soils at the South wash much more readily than soils of similar origin in the Northern States, although it is not known just why this is so. It is largely due, no doubt, to the clean cultivation necessary for the cotton crop, from which all grass and weeds of every kind are scrupulously excluded. The land is thus left practically bare of vegetation for a considerable portion of the year. Gneiss soils, which at the North would be covered with wheat or a permanent sod of grass, are here washed and gullied in cotton culture unless protected by terracing or side hill ditches. On several of the soil formations in South Carolina it is one of the serious problems with which the cotton planter has to deal to prevent his land from being washed and gullied under the continued clean cultivation of cotton. The rivers everywhere within this region are very muddy. The sediment consists, as the planters well know, of the finest and most fertile portions of their soils and of the fertilizers they have applied to the soil for the benefit of their own crops. This is the material of which the present rice soils are formed, and of which every year there is a fresh coating left on the rice lands.

The soil of the rice lands is a very strong clay, containing from 20 to 50 per cent of organic matter so thoroughly disintegrated as to have lost all of its original structure and existing as an amorphous or humus-like mass. In its usual moist or wet condition the soil can be cut with ease like butter or soft cheese, and a stick can be pushed down into it to a very considerable depth. Cultivation is usually done by oxen instead of mules or horses, as they are less likely to mire and can take better care of themselves.

In upland culture the soil is to provide standing room for the crop and to regulate the water supply by conserving the rainfall as well as to supply food materials to the plants. In rice culture an abundance of water is supplied, but in this, as in upland culture, the soils must be well drained so as to supply plenty of air to the roots of the crop. The lands are very close and are usually saturated with water, so that no air can enter except that dissolved in the water itself. There is little chance here for the oxidation of the organic matter of the soil, as it is protected by the limited supply of air. The rice lands are generally underlaid, at a depth of 4 to 6 feet, with an impervious layer of bog iron ore. When there is insufficient air in the soil, as when the soil is saturated under a very shallow layer of water which has not been changed for some time, red, oily scum comes to the surface, as is often seen with stagnant water. These are called "alum" spots by the laborers, and the plants are killed if there is much of it. It shows that there is an insufficient supply of air in the soil and a deoxidation of the iron compounds and of the organic matter in the soil to provide oxygen for the oxidation of other matters. The remedy is to repeatedly ebb and flow the land with every tide, thus letting on successive quantities of fresh, aerated water. The planters are always careful to prevent the water over their rice lands from becoming stagnant, and they frequently have to ebb and flow the land a number of times to replenish the supply of air in the soil. For this reason also it is essential that the drains and canals be kept open, and that they be of sufficient depth to give considerable fall and good drainage, to drain the land properly when the water is let off of the field.

It is this insufficient supply of air in the soil which makes it difficult to get a stand of the finer grasses or of other crops on these very fertile rice lands. The native grasses grow most luxuriantly and form a dense mass of foliage when left undisturbed, but they are very rank and hard and are quite worthless when cut for fodder. Probably if these lands were underlaid with tile, so that they could be more perfectly drained when the water is withdrawn from the field, better grasses could be introduced, which, when properly cared for and judiciously irrigated, would yield enormous crops.

The rice lands must be plowed very shallow, as the subsoil is distinctly poisonous when any considerable amount is turned upon the soil, and it may take several years for the land to recover from a single deep plowing. This is probably because in the complete absence of air in the saturated subsoil the denitrifying organisms, which are active only in the absence of air, would be particularly abundant, and the poisonous alkaloids, closely allied to strychnine, such, for example, as "indole" and "skatole," which are known to be decomposition products resulting from their action, would accumulate in the subsoil to such an extent as to be poisonous to the nitrifying organisms in the soil. This has been shown to be the case in upland soils, and probably explains the fact long held by practical farmers that when too much of the subsoil, at least of certain soil formations, is turned up in deep plowing it "poisons the land." These poisonous alkaloids have been actually separated from an upland subsoil, and it has been shown that they were present in sufficient quantities to at least arrest the action of the nitrifying bacteria in the soil. The conditions are so much more favorable for the formation of these poisonous substances in the subsoil of the rice lands that it can hardly be doubted that they would accumulate in considerable quantities, and that the subsoil actually does "poison the land" when quantities of it are turned up, as claimed by the rice planters.

The use of water in rice culture is to assist in the cultivation of the rice by keeping down grasses and weeds by keeping them wholly immersed in water. If the crown or growing part of the plant be kept continually immersed in water the plant will die, whether it be a grass or a rice plant. In rice culture the rice gets a start of the grass and grows off quicker, and if then the water be maintained above the crown of the grass plant, but below the crown of the rice, the grass is subdued. If, on the contrary, the water be maintained below the crown of the grass or weeds, and the rice be continuously submerged, the rice would be subdued and killed, while the grass would thrive under the treatment. The whole art of the use of water in the cultivation of rice is then to assist in the cultivation and to subdue the grass and weeds in the manner stated. At the same time the details of this cultivation must be arranged to suit the needs of the crop. The rice plant must never be completely submerged, except for a short period in the early life of the plant when a submergence of several days is supposed to stretch the plant upwards and at other times in the growth of the crop for a day or two at a time to kill insects which are becoming very destructive. At the same time, also, the water must not be allowed to become stagnant and must be changed at rather frequent intervals to admit air to the soil in the well aerated water of the river.

In upland culture the texture of a soil and its physical properties very often determine the development of a crop and the relation of the soil to crop production. The soil must conserve the rainfall and maintain a sufficient supply of water at all times for the plant. On an average, rain falls on every third day throughout the year, but in reality this often comes in heavy and prolonged showers, followed by a long period of bright, sunny weather. The soil must conserve this water and maintain a steady and nearly uniform supply for the needs of the plant throughout this rainless period. As a rule, soils can maintain a sufficient amount of water for the needs of plants best adapted to them for a week or ten days, after which the supply must be replenished by a shower of rain. In a good growing season there is a good soaking rain every week or ten days, followed by a period of sunny days. Soils differ, however, in the amount of moisture they can maintain for the crop under these existing climatic conditions. There is, on the average, about 50 per cent of space within the soil into which this water may enter. In a heavy clay soil the grains of sand and clay are extremely small and there is a vast number of them in a cubic foot, and the spaces between the grains are so extremely small that the water moves downward very slowly through the soil. Such a soil will maintain a relatively large and abundant supply of water. The conditions would be favorable for a large leaf development, and the plant would be inclined to be late in coming to maturity. On the other hand, a coarse, sandy soil will have relatively large grains and there will be relatively few of them, so that the spaces between the grains will be relatively large and water will pass downward through such a soil with great ease, so that the soil can not maintain a very abundant supply of water for the crop. The drier conditions in such a soil will be more favorable to the fruiting and early maturity of a plant, and the plant itself will be lighter and more delicate in structure than the same crop grown on a clay soil. The conditions in these two types of land, arising from their difference in texture, are therefore distinctly favorable to different classes of plants.

In rice culture an abundance of water is supplied at all times and the soil is not called on to conserve and maintain this water supply, except for the short periods of dry growth, which hardly amount to more than fifteen or twenty days in the aggregate in the entire period of growth. Nevertheless the texture of the soil is recognized as of very great importance in rice culture, especially in unfavorable seasons, when from continued wet weather or from continued dry weather and salt water the lands can not be properly drained and the water changed. If the land is too close and the movement of water within it too slow, it will not properly drain when the water is withdrawn and there will be no sufficient replacement by the fresh, aërated water of the river. On the other hand, if the lands are too open, whether by sand or organic matter, the soluble matters will be quickly leached out, and in a few years the land will become exhausted and will require attention to bring back its original fertility. For this purpose fertilizers are frequently used, but there is nothing so good as to let the water ebb and flow over the land during a season to deposit a fresh quantity of sediment, which in some unexplained way seems to change the whole character of the land and improve its condition under cultivation. The conditions are not as constant in these open, porous lands and the plant is subjected to more sudden and extreme changes in the course of cultivation, which are decidedly unfavorable.

In upland soils the amount of organic matter varies from a fraction of 1 per cent to about 3 or 4 per cent, rarely exceeding this figure in arable lands, at least in the older agricultural regions of the country. If such soils, containing as much clay as these rice lands, were plowed and cultivated while thoroughly wet and saturated, as these rice lands are, it would render them entirely unfit for subsequent cultivation. The rice lands, however, have from 18 to 50 per cent of organic matter, and this certainly must in some way immure them from injury when cultivated in the condition in which they are usually worked. The soils when completely dried in the laboratory are as hard as rocks, but on moistening the lumps they fall to pieces very completely into the same soft, butter-like mass of their fresh state.

In the upland soils the amount of organic matter usually present in the older agricultural lands does not vary much, and the relation of soils to water is largely dependent, therefore, upon the relative amount and arrangement of the grains of sand and clay. Over large areas of the States bordering the Atlantic coast the relation of the soils to plant development and the local distribution or adaptation of crops appears to be closely dependent upon the amount of clay or of very fine material, smaller than 0.005 mm. in diameter, contained in the soil. It has been shown that the approximate number of grains of sand and clay in a unit volume of soil can be calculated from the mechanical analysis, and that this will show the relative agricultural value of the land if other conditions are normal; in other words, that the texture of the land has more effect upon the development and yield of crops than the actual amount of plant food the soil contains. If the conditions of moisture and heat are favorable to the best development of the plant, the crop can, in general, gather all the food it requires from nearly all soils. In rice soils the large amount of organic matter would greatly modify the physical conditions of the soil.

ANALYSES OF SOILS.

A number of samples of typical rice soils were collected from the large plantation of Mr. R. J. Donaldson, Georgetown, S. C., which are believed to represent fairly well the important types of rice lands of that locality. A considerable number of samples have been collected from other localities in this and in other States, but there has been no opportunity to make a thorough examination of these samples in time for this bulletin. A mechanical analysis has been made of the samples collected from Mr. Donaldson's place and the results certainly seem to explain some of the peculiarities mentioned in the description of these soils.

The mechanical analysis was made by Osborne's "beaker method," and the diameters, given in millimeters, show the range in size of the different grades of sand, silt, and clay into which the soil is divided in the course of the analysis. The most important group in the case of upland soils is the "clay" group, as the grains of clay are so extremely small that there is an enormous number of them. The number of grains in this group is so large that it practically determines the extent of subdivision of the space within the soil in which water is held. It has been found in the upland soils of South Carolina and of Maryland that, under the prevailing climatic conditions, a soil must contain at least 20 per cent of clay to be "strong enough" for a good wheat land. Soils containing less clay than this are excellent for the light-colored tobaccos and for fruit and early truck, but they are rather too light in texture for the economical production of wheat. The very finest wheat lands contain from 30 to 35 per cent of clay. Under the prevailing climatic conditions the soil must contain at least 25 or 30 per cent of clay for a good grass land, and soils containing less clay than this are too light in texture for a permanent sod of grass. Limestone soils, like the Cumberland Valley and the famous "blue grass lands," have from 40 to 50 per cent of clay.

These rice lands can not be compared in this respect with the upland soils, for the large amount of organic matter must greatly modify the simple structure of the soil grains, and besides the soil itself is not called upon to maintain a supply of water for the plant, although it must still provide good drainage and a sufficient circulation of air.

The following tables show the relative amounts of the different grades of sand, silt, and clay in these typical lowland rice lands, calculated on an air-dry basis and also on an organic and water-free basis. The latter results offer a better basis for comparing the structure of these soils with the structure of upland soils, and it will be seen that if the organic matter were removed, as it will be through oxidation in the course of time when the lands are higher and drier than they are at present, they would be exceedingly strong clay soils.

No analyses have been made of rice lands taken from farther up the rivers, but it is probable that such lands, being nearer the up-country where the sediment is derived, would have relatively more sand and silt and less clay than these soils taken from near the mouth of the river and just above the salt water. These soils are considered the very best and finest type of rice lands in the State.

TABLE V.—*Mechanical analysis of rice lands.*

[Air-dry samples.]

Diameter.	Conventional names.	26. Big Cypress soil. 0-6 inches.	24. Cooter field soil, 0-6 inches.	25. Sob field soil, 0-6 inches.	24b. Cooter field subsoil, 6-9 inches.	25b. Sob field subsoil, 6-9 inches.
mm.						
2- 1	Fine gravel	0.00	0.00	0.00	0.00	0.00
1-. 5	Coarse sand	0.00	0.00	0.71	0.00	0.08
.5-. 25	Medium sand	0.05	0.10	2.70	0.00	0.25
.25-. 1	Fine sand	0.06	0.11	0.83	0.04	0.13
.1-. 05	Very fine sand	2.56	1.03	0.37	3.50	0.15
.05-. 01	Silt	26.38	19.65	10.92	21.12	13.97
.01-. 005	Fine silt	8.43	10.83	5.32	12.95	8.10
.005-.0001	Clay	46.15	43.70	31.90	43.49	34.85
	Total mineral matter ..	83.63	75.42	52.15	81.10	57.53
	Organic matter, water, loss	16.37	24.58	47.85	18.90	42.47
		100.00	100.00	100.00	100.00	100.00
	Loss by direct ignition.	18.68	24.82	47.36	17.22	39.05

TABLE VI.—*Mechanical analysis of rice lands.*

[Calculated on organic and water-free basis.]

Diameter.	Conventional names.	26. Big Cypress soil. 0-6 inches.	24. Cooter field soil, 0-6 inches.	25. Sob field soil, 0-6 inches.	24b. Cooter field subsoil, 6-9 inches.	25b. Sob field subsoil, 6-9 inches.
mm.						
2-1	Fine gravel	0.00	0.00	0.00	0.00	0.00
1-. 5	Coarse sand	0.00	0.00	1.36	0.00	0.14
.5-. 25	Medium sand	0.06	0.13	5.18	0.00	0.43
.25-. 1	Fine sand	0.07	0.15	1.59	0.06	0.23
.1-. 05	Very fine sand	3.05	1.36	0.71	4.32	0.26
.05-. 01	Silt	31.55	26.05	19.79	26.04	24.30
.01-. 005	Fine silt	10.05	14.36	10.20	15.97	14.09
.005 . 0001	Clay	55.22	57.95	61.17	53.61	60.65
		100.00	100.00	100.00	100.00	100.00

(26) *Big cypress field, "clay and alluvial mud."*—When this sample was taken the water had been off the field for a short time and the land was being prepared for seeding. The soil was very soft and sticky. It could be readily cut like soft butter. This is considered the very finest type of rice land, and such soil as this can be cropped indefinitely without showing any effect of the continued cropping. It will stand more hard farming and the crop is more uniform and more reliable than on any other type of rice land. It will be seen from the tables that this has relatively more clay in the air-dry sample than the others, and it has only 18.68 per cent of loss on ignition, principally organic matter. When calculated upon an organic and water-free basis this soil contains about 55.22 per cent of clay, and in the normal condition of a well-drained upland soil it would contain about 50 per cent of clay and would have about the same texture as a heavy limestone soil.

(24) *Cooter field.*—The water had been off of this field about twenty-four hours before the sample was taken, and only one tide had been over it then. The soil was black and sticky, and was full of roots

and stubble. The subsoil was a light yellow color; but this could not be sampled lower than 9 inches, as water rose freely into the hole at this depth. This soil is a typical rice soil, and is about as good as that from the "Big Cypress" field. It can be cropped indefinitely as the other can, but it is hardly as reliable in unfavorable seasons. It will be seen from the table that this soil has more clay when the analysis is calculated on the organic and water-free basis, but there is also a greater loss on ignition (24.32 per cent), and there is consequently less clay and more organic matter in the air-dry sample than in the last case.

(25) *Sob field.*—This is a typical swamp bog or peat, and represents a large class of bay lands. As the name implies, it is soggy and shakes for a considerable distance around any pressure on the surface, as in walking. These lands are naturally poor, and are considered the very poorest kind of rice lands. They are exhausted in two or three years, and require rest to produce good crops. They respond readily to commercial fertilizers, and one year's rest with the deposit from the river in the continual ebb and flow of the tide gives splendid crops. It is not known to what the rapid deterioration of these lands is due. It can certainly not be due to an actual loss of plant food, but it must probably be due to some physical change in the structure of the land which interferes with the proper drainage or aëration of the soil, changes which have been brought about by the process of cultivation and which are corrected by the effect of fertilizers or the natural deposits from the river on the texture of the soil. It would be interesting to determine what changes do occur to account for the rapid deterioration of these lands, and this could readily be done. It will be seen from the tables that this soil gave 47.36 per cent of loss on ignition, indicating a very large amount of organic matter. The air-dried sample contained only 31.90 per cent of clay and only 52.15 per cent of total mineral matter. Calculated on an organic- and water-free basis, this soil contains over 61 per cent of clay. The very large amount of organic matter contained in this soil is evidently unfavorable to the growth of rice, and the very presence of so much organic matter probably indicates poor drainage and a very limited supply of air, which would otherwise have oxidized the organic matter, and these are conditions which we have seen to be unfavorable for the proper development of rice.

These three samples represent, it is believed, the most important types of lowland rice lands in South Carolina, representing the finest and poorest types of land in that important locality near the coast where it is considered the very finest rice lands are to be found. These analyses seem to show an important influence of the texture of these soils, and the relative amount of sand, clay, and organic matter which they contain, to the production of rice. If this line of investigation were followed out, and the structure of the rice soils from a number of localities was carefully studied, it would probably have an important practical bearing upon the selection, cultivation, and manuring of rice lands.

UPLAND RICE SOILS.

As stated in another part of this report, upland rice can be grown on any soil adapted to wheat or cotton, where the ordinary climatic conditions are favorable. The lands best adapted to cotton and wheat, under the meteorological conditions which prevail in South Carolina, have from 20 to 40 per cent of clay, and for both of these crops the land must be perfectly well drained and there must be free access of air to the roots of the plant. Rice will thrive with a more limited supply of air in the soil, and for obvious reasons upland rice is preferably grown on low, wet spots, where neither cotton nor wheat could be successfully grown. These areas are usually underlaid with an impervious clay, or for some other reason have insufficient drainage, and the soils are very constantly wet, although there is commonly no water standing over the surface. A limited supply of air favors the accumulation of a large amount of organic matter in the soil.

The following table gives the mechanical analysis of a typical soil of this kind from Lenoir County, N. C.:

TABLE VII.—*Mechanical analysis of rice lands.*

[S. G. Wooten, Lagrange. Lenoir County, N. C.]

Diameter.	Conventional names.	Air-dry samples.		Organic free basis.	
		0-6 inches.	6-12 inches.	0-6 inches.	6-12 inches.
Mm.					
2-1	Fine gravel	0.00	0.05	0.00	0.08
1-.5	Coarse sand	0.39	0.31	0.52	0.50
.5-.25	Medium sand	1.70	1.60	2.28	2.72
.25-.1	Fine sand	6.79	3.13	9.09	5.04
.1-.05	Very fine sand	13.43	9.62	17.98	15.50
.05-.01	Silt	17.36	13.77	23.25	22.18
.01-.005	Fine silt	5.13	3.05	6.87	4.91
.005-.0001	Clay	29.88	30.46	40.01	49.07
		74.68	62.08	100.00	100.00
Organic matter, water, loss		25.32	37.92		
		100.00	100.00		
Loss by direct ignition		24.39	34.64		

It will be seen that there are 24.39 per cent and 34.64 per cent of loss on ignition, respectively, in the soil and subsoil, or about as much, on an average, as in the lowland rice soils of South Carolina. This indicates a large amount of organic matter in this soil, and this accumulation of organic matter indicates a very limited supply of air. The analysis based on the organic and water-free basis shows this land to contain about 40 and 49 per cent of clay, respectively, in the soil and subsoil, which would be regarded as a very strong clay land for other staple crops under better drainage and a more normal amount of organic matter.

The following table gives the mechanical analysis of a soil near Sumter, S. C., very similar to the above, but probably not so good for rice:

TABLE VIII.—*Mechanical analysis of rice land.*

[Sumter, S. C.]

Diameter.	Conventional names.	0-12 inches.
mm.		
2-1	Fine gravel..............	0.15
1-.5	Coarse sand	1.39
.5-.25	Medium sand..........	7.65
.25-.1	Fine sand..............	10.16
.1-.05	Very fine sand.........	17.41
.05 .01	Silt......................	21.10
.01-.005	Fine silt................	5.25
.005-.0001	Clay	22.88
		85.99
Organic matter, water, loss		14.01
		100.00
Loss by direct ignition		17.05

This soil is shown to have about 17 per cent of loss on ignition and about 22.88 per cent of clay. A crop of maize had just been gathered from this land when the sample was taken. The crop had been raised on high beds or ridges similar to those used on the Sea Islands and partaking somewhat of the nature of the old Roman beds, and for the same purpose, to secure good drainage and a freer circulation of air in the soil. The ridges were 18 to 20 inches high from the bottom of the alley to the top of the ridge and about 5 feet across at the base of the ridge. The crop was planted on top of this ridge and it was in comparatively well-drained soil, but with an abundant and constant supply of moisture in the saturated subsoil below the ridge, and large crops of corn could be thus produced.